D0831151

THE MARSHALL PLAN

*German worker is helping to lay the foundation for one of the
low-cost housing projects financed by the Marshall Plan.*

THE MARSHALL PLAN

AND THE SHAPING OF AMERICAN STRATEGY

BRUCE JONES

EDITOR

With a foreword by
STROBE TALBOTT

BROOKINGS INSTITUTION PRESS
Washington, D.C.

Copyright © 2017
THE BROOKINGS INSTITUTION
1775 Massachusetts Avenue, N.W., Washington, D.C. 20036
www.brookings.edu

The Brookings Institution is a private nonprofit organization devoted to research, education, and publication on important issues of domestic and foreign policy. Its principal purpose is to bring the highest quality independent research and analysis to bear on current and emerging policy problems. Interpretations or conclusions in Brookings publications should be understood to be solely those of the authors.

Library of Congress Cataloging-in-Publication data are available.
ISBN 978-0-8157-2953-2 (cloth: alk. paper)
ISBN 978-0-8157-2954-9 (ebook)

9 8 7 6 5 4 3 2

Typeset in Bembo

Composition by Elliott Beard

CONTENTS

THE MARSHALL PLAN

BROOKINGS IN WAR AND PEACE

Strobe Talbott

The European Recovery Program, commonly known as the Marshall Plan, was a pivotal undertaking in America's emergence as a global power and a protector of its fellow democracies on the far side of the Atlantic. Winston Churchill famously hailed it as "the most unsordid act in history." The historian Norman Davies was less grandiloquent but more to the point in identifying the motive behind the U.S. investment of $13 billion in the rehabilitation of European economies: he called it "an act of the most enlightened self-interest in history."

With the wisdom of hindsight, the Marshall Plan deserves another accolade. By transforming a wartime alliance into a transatlantic community based on shared interests and values that was the bedrock of the world order for decades to come, it was a stunning and sustained success and an exemplar for American foreign policy in the future.

We at Brookings have an institutional interest in the Marshall Plan, since our predecessors were involved in refining it and helping a Democratic administration shepherd it through a Republican-controlled Congress. We regard our Institution's contribution to that process as an iconic example of our ethos, which includes nonpartisanship, and our mission, which is the improvement of governance. Hence, as we reflect on Brookings's legacy in its centenary year, the publication of this book.

Our institution was the world's first independent public policy research organization. Its birth and maturation coincided with America's emergence as a decisive actor on the world stage—and, in particular, on the battlefields of the two world wars.

In November 1914 our founding trustees drew up the articles of corporation for what would become the Brookings Institution during the last days of the first Battle of Ypres; in March 1916 they drafted a public prospectus while the Battle of Verdun was raging; and they opened for business in October of that year, five months before President Woodrow Wilson sent the American soldiers "over there."

Four months later, Wilson appointed the vice chair of our board, Robert S. Brookings—a business-

man, educator, and philanthropist from St. Louis—to the War Industries Board. The experience convinced Brookings that sound public and national security policy required a robust partnership between government and the private sector.

In the 1920s several of our scholars focused on European recovery from the Great War. During that decade, Robert S. Brookings assumed board leadership of the institution that came to bear his name. In 1926, six years before his death, he published a pamphlet laying out his vision of a European economic union.[1]

During the 1930s Brookings scholars grappled with the monetary strains in the Great Depression and, once that crisis was over, the challenge of creating a stable, open global economy based on international political cooperation. Leading much of that work was Leo Pasvolsky, an early recruit who earned a Ph.D. in economics from the graduate school that was part of the Institution in its early years. He also became the first of our scholars to pass back and forth numerous times through the revolving door between Brookings and the U.S. government, with stints in the Commerce and State departments. In early 1941 Pasvolsky accepted a full-time job, primarily as an adviser to Secretary of State Cordell Hull, at the level of an assistant secretary while keeping in close though informal touch with Brookings president Harold Moulton.

After Pearl Harbor, the Institution aligned its

agenda with yet another war effort. From their offices on Lafayette Square, less than two hundred yards from the White House lawn, our scholars produced reports on how to meet the manpower needs of mobilization, ensure electrical power for the manufacture of armaments, and boost the production of gasoline, tires, and automobiles for the Army. Other projects included advice to Canada and Great Britain on rationing, subsidies, and price controls, as well as an assessment of German manpower as a measure of how long the Nazi war machine could remain on the offensive.

As early as the grim year of 1942, the Institution was already looking toward eventual victory. It published a book by Arthur Millspaugh—a political scientist, economist, and diplomat who had close ties to Brookings and Moulton—titled *Peace Plans and American Choices: The Pros and Cons of World Order.* The first option was something of a straw man: an "America on its own" that would simultaneously "assume international responsibilities" while "avoiding direct and formal commitments or entanglements outside this Hemisphere," a contradiction that Millspaugh clearly saw as a fatal flaw. The second was a British-American alliance at the core of a "Union of Democracies" that would cooperate with the yet-to-be-formed United Nations. The third was a global network of regional arrangements ("alliances, leagues, customs unions, security pacts"). Millspaugh saw virtues and compatibilities in both. He concluded with a chapter on whether there should be a "cooling-off" period after the war, in which the combatants would concentrate on their home fronts rather than on grand internationalist undertakings. Millspaugh ended with an emphatic rejection of that idea: "War creates among people a growing feeling of revulsion against itself. Satiated with excitement, anxiety, and horror, people come to feel that no price is too high to pay for peace. The most favorable time, therefore, to crystallize opinion on the question of world order would seem to be during the war; and the best time, apparently, to win popular approval for a comprehensive settlement is immediately after the war. 'There is a tide in the affairs of men.'"[2]

In addition to U.S. leadership, the world and America itself needed a universally representative organization to serve as the architecture of a lasting peace. In 1943, Pasvolsky, from his position at the right hand of Secretary Hull, was the principal drafter of the United Nations Charter. The UN's most powerful body, the Security Council, would consist of a small inner circle of permanent members including the big three (the United States, the United Kingdom, and the Soviet Union), each with a veto over any "substantive" resolution. This feature would soon be a reminder that creating permanent arrangements without a crystal ball can also create long-lasting difficulties.[3]

As the Third Reich crumbled in 1945, another totalitarian empire laid the ground for territorial gains westward, initially and ignominiously with American and British acquiescence. Meeting in Yalta that February, the "big three" victors—Franklin Roosevelt, Churchill, and Joseph Stalin—formally carved up the map of Europe, consigning much of its East to nearly a half century of subjugation.

While the U.S. government was accommodating Stalin's expansionism, many Americans, including members of Congress, were transferring their vigilance from Nazis in their midst to Soviet fellow travelers and spies. The House Un-American Activities Committee (HUAC) was already a bellwether of the Red Scare and the McCarthy years: it had been ferreting out suspected Soviet sympathizers since its inception in 1938. After V-E Day in May 1945, HUAC was elevated from a "special" committee that convened intermittently to a more powerful standing one. One of its most zealous Republican members, Karl Mundt of South Dakota, asked Moulton for Brookings's advice on "the standards by which its conduct might be guided."

When Brookings's senior research librarian, Sarah Chilton, brought this document and its provenance to my attention, I was curious to see how our predecessors responded. They produced a public report that was an unwavering, unambiguous warning against witch hunts of the sort that the committee would conduct in the years ahead. Rather than advising HUAC what it should do, the authors, Lewis Meriam and Harold Metz, focused on what it should not do. The limits of the committee's writ, they argued, derived from the Constitution itself and, in particular, the First Amendment. "It is un-American," they wrote, "for any person or association of persons"—a formulation that, in context, clearly included agencies of the Executive Branch and committees of the Congress—"to deprive any individual or group of individuals of any of [the] rights with which government itself cannot constitutionally interfere."

As for the growing Soviet menace itself, Brookings scholars, like some officials in the State Department, floated ideas based on the premise of Yalta: Roosevelt's and Churchill's illusion that the postwar order could include accommodation of Stalin's determination to extend the U.S.S.R.'s "sphere of influence," which was, in fact, a sphere of domination. A Brookings book suggested a joint "Big Three Commission" to supervise the reconstruction of Iran that might nudge Moscow toward cooperation with its wartime allies.[4]

But Stalin was far more interested in conquest than condominiums. In January 1947 the Kremlin orchestrated a sham election in Poland that brought communists to power through the use of intimidation and violence.

President Harry Truman recognized the escalation of the threat and decided to make a change at the State Department. He removed James Byrnes, a former member of Congress and Supreme Court justice who had succeeded Hull as secretary of state, and in his place appointed General George Marshall.

Marshall was already on the record as an advocate of a robust American effort to lift civilian populations out of the rubble. "The world of suffering people looks to us for leadership," he had said two years earlier. "Their thoughts, however, are not concentrated alone on this problem. They have more immediate and terribly pressing concerns where the mouthful of food will come from, where they will find shelter tonight, and where they will find warmth. Along with the great problem of maintaining the peace we must solve the problem of the pittance of food, of clothing and coal and homes. Neither of these problems can be solved alone."

Marshall made that statement in November 1945, the very month he made his transition from warrior to diplomat. Truman had sent him to China to assess the civil war between the nationalists and communists and its implications for American interests. "Marshall is the greatest man of World War II," Truman wrote in his diary when he selected Marshall as secretary of state. "He managed to get along with Roosevelt, the

Congress, Churchill, the Navy and the Joint Chiefs of Staff and he made a grand record in China. When I asked him to [be] my special envoy to China, he merely said, 'Yes, Mr. President I'll go.' No argument only patriotic action. And if any man was entitled to balk and ask for a rest, he was. We'll have a real State Department now."

The U.S. ambassador in Moscow, Walter Bedell ("Beetle") Smith, wasted no time in sending a private message to his new boss and former comrade-in-arms. Both were soldiers in civvies who had worked closely during the war. As chief of staff to Dwight Eisenhower, the supreme commander of Allied Forces in Europe, Smith had accepted the surrender of the German High Command. Marshall, as chief of staff of the U.S. Army from 1939 through 1945, had been Eisenhower's commanding officer. While much of the world's attention was on the Kremlin-manipulated virtual coup in Poland, Smith was focused on Stalin's ambitions further to the west—in occupied Germany. In his message to Marshall, Smith allowed himself a bit of mordant humor in conveying a deadly serious warning: "There are signs that the dream of happy union between Soviet resources and manpower and German technical skill and administrative ability is again hovering about [the] pillows of Soviet leaders."

Meanwhile, America's staunchest ally, Great Britain, had staggered into 1947 under the blows of Mother Nature. One of the coldest winters on record forced

Britons to dig their way out of serial blizzards, which overtaxed an electrical grid that was already stressed by the war and triggered a fuel crisis that jeopardized the country's chance for an economic rebound. On top of that, Churchill, the great hero of the war and champion of Britain's role as a world power, had been voted out of office and was now in the opposition. Whitehall and Westminster were under the control of the Labour Party, which was preoccupied with the desperate needs on the home front and consciously reeling back Britain's commitments abroad.

That January, as the geopolitical horizon darkened, there was a consequential shift in the correlation of forces in American domestic politics. The midterm elections of the previous November had ended fourteen years of the Democratic Party's control of the Senate and the House of Representatives. A major factor in the reversal was the sudden ascendancy to the presidency of Harry Truman, an untested successor to FDR. When the 80th Congress took over the Capitol, the administration had to confront the Soviet menace with a strategy that would have support from both parties.

In March 1947 Truman went before the two houses of Congress to proclaim the doctrine that would bear his name: America was committed to countering Soviet aggression and coercion, starting with emergency aid to bolster two countries, Greece and Turkey, in order to prevent them from falling within the U.S.S.R.'s sphere of domination.

A month later, Truman's high-profile adviser, Bernard Baruch, delivered a speech featuring the phrase "cold war," which Walter Lippmann then popularized. It had a salient origin. A year-and-a-half earlier, George Orwell had written an essay on the implications of America's incineration of Hiroshima and Nagasaki with atomic bombs. Orwell foresaw "a permanent state of 'cold war' . . . 'a peace that is no peace'" but better than a nuclear Armageddon.

Marshall, like Truman himself, had absorbed that stark reality. He was seized of the imperative that, for decades to come, the supreme responsibility of the United States would be keeping the new war cold.

America's strategy for waging the cold war was a classic example of using "soft power" (economic, cultural, and ideological strength) in tandem with "hard power" (military force) more than four decades before that dualism became part of the vocabulary of U.S. foreign and security policy.[5] Hard power would take the form of the North Atlantic Treaty Organization (NATO), created in 1949, and other anti-Soviet alliances as well as the American nuclear deterrent.

Initially, however, the implementation of the Truman doctrine relied heavily on soft power. As the president said in his address to Congress, Greece was vulnerable to a Soviet takeover because its governing institutions and economy were weak. Therefore the U.S. government should provide "American administrators, economists, and technicians to insure that the financial and other aid given to Greece shall be used effectively in creating a stable and self-sustaining economy and in improving its public administration." He made much the same case for Turkey, saying, "Should we fail to aid Greece and Turkey in this fateful hour, the effect will be far reaching to the West as well as to the East."

The Greek-Turkish aid package was an emergency measure. What the United States needed next was a far more expansive, long-range, and heftier commitment to Western Europe as a whole.

Marshall went public with the outlines of just such an initiative on June 5, 1947, at Harvard, where he received an honorary degree. The address was devoid of lofty oratory, and the delivery was sober. After thanking the university's president, James B. Conant, and the other degree recipients, Marshall, standing on the steps of Memorial Church in Harvard Yard, introduced his announcement of the European Recovery Program by saying, "I need not tell you gentlemen that the world situation is very serious." He then pledged that America would do "whatever it is able" to restore its "normal economic health." Otherwise there could be "no political stability and no assured peace" in the world.

The following day, the press coverage included a

New York Times article under the headline "France Is Stirred by Marshall Plan."

The moniker stuck. Six years later, after the completion of the plan and Marshall's retirement from public service, he would receive the Nobel Peace Prize.

Marshall was heavily influenced by a seminal document of the cold war, George Kennan's "Long Telegram," written in 1946 from the U.S. embassy in Moscow, where he was in charge following the departure of W. Averell Harriman as ambassador. Marshall early in 1947 had asked Kennan to set up a strategic planning staff reporting directly to the secretary of state. Marshall's Harvard speech was drafted by Charles ("Chip") Bohlen, a renowned Soviet specialist, who drew from Kennan's cable and subsequent internal memoranda assessing the Kremlin's goals and recommendations on U.S. policy. In July, a month after the announcement of the Marshall Plan, an amplified version of the Long Telegram appeared in *Foreign Affairs*, the journal of the Council on Foreign Relations, under the title "Sources of Soviet Conduct" and the byline "X." The attempt at anonymity failed almost immediately because Kennan's telegram had been circulated widely in Washington.

Kennan's policy proscription was encapsulated in a single sentence: Soviet expansionism must "be contained by the adroit and vigilant application of counterforce at a series of constantly shifting geographical and political points."

In the months, years, and decades to come there would be an ongoing debate over how to balance military deterrence with the parallel effort to restore and sustain economic vitality and democratic governance in nations on the periphery of the expanding Soviet camp.

The Marshall Plan put an emphasis on the latter challenge. Without a jumpstart in European recovery, the Soviet juggernaut might be irresistible, threatening the war-ravaged democracies of Western Europe. Secretary of State Marshall—and, more to the point, *General* Marshall—was the most effective possible promoter of putting a premium on the economic and political health of countries that were targets of the Kremlin.[6]

Brookings was directly involved in the follow-up to the Harvard speech. In July Truman appointed Moulton to a committee, chaired by Commerce Secretary Harriman, to advise the executive branch on how to disburse the aid package "safely and wisely."[7]

Throughout the summer and into the fall, Marshall remained a powerful advocate. Truman asked wryly, "Can you imagine [the plan's] chances of passage in an election year in a Republican congress if it is named for Truman and not Marshall?"

On the last day of the year, the Republican chair

of the Senate Committee on Foreign Relations, Arthur Vandenberg of Michigan, requested Moulton to charge Brookings scholars with preparing an analysis of the plan and proposals on its implementation, which Vandenberg saw as the government's "biggest single conundrum." He turned to Moulton because "the deep and universal respect which the Brookings Institution richly deserves and enjoys would make your recommendation of tremendous value to those of us who are struggling in the trenches." He added privately, in a letter to Moulton, that the committee "could have advice from no source which could be of greater value or command more general respect."

Moulton asked all of his more than thirty fellow scholars to give highest priority to the task. The finished report was submitted to Vandenberg on January 22, 1948. As soon as it arrived on his desk, he gave it a quick and appreciative read and released it to the press, trumpeting it as just the advice that he and the committee needed.

The report reinforced the Harriman committee's view that responsibility for the plan should be assigned to a new, autonomous agency in the executive branch, the Economic Cooperation Administration, directly under the president, thereby maximizing its authority within the government and its ability to call on the necessary resources.

The role of the Brookings Institution was widely noted in the press and lauded publicly by Vandenberg as a "highly important service." When the report was reviewed, Vandenberg said in a speech on the Senate floor that the U.S. government had a "great obligation to the Brookings Institution for the masterly job it did. The provisions in the pending bill largely follow its recommendations."

In less than three months, Congress approved the program. Seventeen nations were its beneficiaries. Within four years, their industrial production leapt by 55 percent. Many Europeans were lifted out of poverty; old and new businesses began to prosper, creating jobs and catalyzing cross-border trade. Pan-European commissions and institutions were established, laying the ground for integration and eventually the European Union.

Leo Pasvolsky, who had returned to Brookings early in 1946 and participated in preparing and drafting the report to Congress, continued to assess the aid program as it took hold. He was the founder of the International Studies Group, the forerunner of Foreign Policy at Brookings today, which he led until his death in 1953.

In the afterword of this book, Pasvolsky's current successor, Bruce Jones, reflects with Will Moreland on an abiding American interest in a free and democratic Europe, the link between international security and economic development, and the importance of American leadership in strengthening regional and global institutions and agreements. All three of these imperatives were embedded in the vision that inspired the Marshall Plan and in the Brookings report to the Senate. They are every bit as vital today and will be for the decades to come.

NOTES

1. *The Proposed European Economic Conferences* was published by Doubleday in 1926.

2. Millspaugh published five other books with the Brookings Institution Press: *Public Welfare Organization* (1935), *Local Democracy and Crime Control* (1936), *Democracy, Efficiency, Stability: An Appraisal of American Government* (1942), *Americans in Persia* (1946), and *Toward Efficient Democracy: The Question of Governmental Organization* (1949).

3. Pasvolsky, while revered by many, inevitably had his detractors on both ends of the political and ideological spectrum. I. F. Stone called him "Kerensky's gift to American foreign policy and political science" and accused him of pushing Brookings research toward "an ultra-right points of view." Dean Acheson, who served as a trustee of Brookings from May 1938 to February 1949 and vice chair from October 1939 until his resignation, knew Pasvolsky not as a scholar but as Cordell Hull's adviser and speechwriter. Acheson had a low opinion of both men. He regarded Hull as something of a dullard and Pasvolsky as a dreamer infatuated with free trade as a panacea to many of the dangers certain to arise after the war. Pasvolsky, who also played a role at the Dumbarton Oaks and San Francisco conferences that laid the foundations for the UN, appears in several belittling passages of Acheson's Pulitzer Prize–winning memoir, *Present at the Creation*; and in a 1967 letter, Acheson referred to "that little rat Leo Pasvolsky's United Nations."

4. *Americans in Persia*, by Arthur Millspaugh, was published by the Brookings Institution in 1946.

5. Joseph Nye, a professor at Harvard University who served in several administrations, was an influential explicator and advocate of soft power. He wrote a book with that title in 1990 and ten years later edited, with John D. Donahue, *Governance in a Globalizing World,* published by the Brookings Institution Press.

6. In 1950 Truman reassigned Marshall to the Pentagon as secretary of defense. Thus the highest ranking soldier in World War II completed his career at the right hand of the commander-in-chief in the cold war.

7. Harriman's mother, Mary Williamson Harriman, was a founding trustee of what became the Brookings Institution.

ONE

THE MARSHALL PLAN SPEECH

For one of the most lauded U.S. foreign policy achievements of the twentieth century, the Marshall Plan began with little fanfare on June 5, 1947. Speaking in Harvard Yard, George C. Marshall offered a decidedly subdued beginning to the European Recovery Program that would eventually bear his name. Though Marshall had become convinced throughout the first half of 1947 of the need for a significant aid package to revitalize Europe, the secretary had no desire for a grandiose launch to the new initiative. Marshall notified no press. He consulted no governments. Even Harvard's president, James Conant, was unaware of the contents of the eleven-minute speech. Yet, in those brief minutes Marshall would outline the depth of the crisis confronting Europe and the need for long-term U.S. assistance and engagement to stabilize the continent. The address marked a milestone in the Truman administration's efforts to sustain the engagement of a war-weary American public.

*General Marshall visits 3rd Division and
receives flowers from French children.*

Mr. President, Dr. Conant, members of the board of overseers, ladies and gentlemen, I'm profoundly grateful and touched by the distinction and honor and great compliment accorded me by the authorities of Harvard this morning. I'm overwhelmed, as a matter of fact, and I'm rather fearful of my inability to maintain such a high rating as you've been generous enough to accord to me. In these historic and lovely surroundings, this perfect day, and this very wonderful assembly, it is a tremendously impressive thing to an individual in my position.

I need not tell you gentlemen that the world situation is very serious. That must be apparent to all intelligent people. I think one difficulty is that the problem is one of such enormous complexity that the very mass of facts presented to the public by press and radio make it exceedingly difficult for the man in the street to reach a clear appraisement of the situation. Furthermore, the people of this country are distant from the troubled areas of the earth and it is hard for them to comprehend the plight and consequent reactions of the long-suffering peoples, and the effect of those reactions on their governments in connection with our efforts to promote peace in the world.

In considering the requirements for the rehabilitation of Europe, the physical loss of life, the visible destruction of cities, factories, mines and railroads was correctly estimated, but it has become obvious during recent months that this visible destruction was probably less serious than the dislocation of the entire fabric of European economy. For the past ten years conditions have been highly abnormal. The feverish preparation for war and the more feverish maintenance of the war effort engulfed all aspects of national economies. Machinery has fallen into disrepair or is entirely obsolete. Under the arbitrary and destructive Nazi rule, virtually every possible enterprise was geared into the German war machine. Long-standing commercial ties, private institutions, banks, insurance companies and shipping companies disappeared, through loss of capital, absorption through nationalization or by simple destruction. In many countries, confidence in the local currency has been severely shaken. The breakdown of the business structure of Europe during the war was complete. Recovery has been seriously retarded by the fact that two years after the close of hostilities a peace settlement with Germany and Austria has not been agreed upon. But even given a more prompt solution of these difficult problems, the rehabilitation of the economic structure of Europe quite evidently will require a much longer time and greater effort than had been foreseen.

There is a phase of this matter which is both interesting and serious. The farmer has always produced the foodstuffs to exchange with the city dweller for the other necessities of life. This division of labor is the basis of modern civilization. At the present time it is threatened with breakdown. The town and city industries are not producing adequate goods to exchange with the food-producing farmer. Raw materials and fuel are in short supply. Machinery is lacking or worn out. The farmer of the peasant cannot find the goods for sale which he desires to purchase. So the sale of his farm produce for money which he cannot use seems to him an unprofitable transaction. He, therefore, has withdrawn many fields from crop cultivation and is using them for grazing. He feeds more grain to stock and finds for himself and his family an ample supply of food, however short he may be on clothing and the other ordinary gadgets of civilization. Meanwhile people in the cities are short of food and fuel. So the governments are forced to use their foreign money and credits to procure these necessities abroad. This process exhausts funds which are urgently needed for reconstruction. This a very serious situation is rapidly developing which bodes no good for the world. The modern system of the division of labor upon which the exchange of products is based is in danger of breaking down.

The truth of the matter is that Europe's requirements for the next three or four years of foreign food and other essential products—principally from America—are so much greater than her present ability to pay that she must have substantial additional help, or face economic, social and political deterioration of a very grave character.

The remedy lies in breaking the vicious circle and restoring the confidence of the European people in the economic future of their own countries and of Europe as a whole. The manufacturer and the farmer throughout wide areas must be able and willing to exchange their products for currencies the continuing value of which is not open to question.

Aside from the demoralizing effect on the world at large and the possibilities of disturbances arising as a result of the desperation of the people concerned, the consequences to the economy of the United States should be apparent to all. It is logical that the United States should do whatever it is able to do to assist in the return of normal economic health in the world, without which there can be no political stability and no assured peace. Our policy is directed not against any country or doctrine but against hunger, poverty, desperation and chaos. Its purpose should be the revival of a working economy in the world so as to permit the emergence of political and social conditions in which free institutions can exist. Such assistance, I am convinced, must not be on a piecemeal basis as various crises develop. Any assistance that this Government may render in the future should provide a cure rather than a mere palliative. Any government that is willing to assist in the task of recovery will find full cooperation, I am sure, on the part of the United States Government. Any government which maneuvers to block the recovery of other countries cannot expect help from us. Furthermore, governments, political parties or groups which seek to perpetuate human misery in order to profit therefrom politically or otherwise will encounter the opposition of the United States.

It is already evident that, before the United States Government can proceed much further in its efforts to alleviate the situation and help start the European world on its way to recovery, there must be some agreement among the countries of Europe as to the requirements of the situation and the part those countries themselves will take in order to give proper effect to whatever action might be undertaken by this Government. It would be neither fitting nor efficacious for this Government to undertake to draw up unilaterally a program designed to place Europe on its feet economically. This is the business of the Europeans. The initiative, I think, must come from Europe. The role of this country should consist of friendly aid in the drafting of a European program and of later support of such a program so far as it may be practical for us to do so. The program should be a joint one, agreed to by a number, if not all European nations.

An essential part of any successful action on the part of the United States is an understanding on the part of the people of America of the character of the problem and the remedies to be applied. Political passion and prejudice should have no part. With foresight, and a willingness on the part of our people to face up to the vast responsibility which history has clearly placed upon our country, the difficulties I have outlined can and will be overcome.

I am sorry that on occasion I have said something publicly in regard to our international situation; I've been forced by the necessities of the case to enter into rather technical discussions. But to my mind, it is of vast importance that our people reach some general understanding of what the complications really are, rather than react from a passion or a prejudice or an emotion of the moment. As I said more formally a moment ago, we are remote from the scene of these troubles. It is virtually impossible at this distance merely by reading, or listening, or even seeing photographs or motion pictures, to grasp at all the real significance of the situation. And yet the whole world of the future hangs on a proper judgment. It hangs, I think, to a large extent on the realization of the American people, of just what are the various dominant factors. What are the reactions of the people? What are the justifications of those reactions? What are the sufferings? What is needed? What can best be done? What must be done? Thank you very much.

TWO

BROOKINGS REPORT FOR THE SENATE FOREIGN RELATIONS COMMITTEE

January 22, 1948

Marshall's Harvard speech may have set a lodestar for American foreign policy, but the hard tasks remained of galvanizing public support and crafting an effective means of implementation. Both started with the U.S. Senate. As outlined in Strobe Talbott's foreword to this volume, Senator Arthur Vandenberg quickly drew Brookings into this venture. On December 31, 1947, he requested of Institution President Harold Moulton a report outlining how best to implement Marshall's vision. Presented to the Foreign Relations Committee only twenty-three days later, the Administration of United States Aid for a European Recovery Program *was a success on both fronts. The document not only laid out the skeleton of the Economic Cooperation Agency that would coordinate and direct the vast resources needed for European recovery, but also was immediately released to the press to allay public skepticism around the project. Though not the first Brookings report of its kind, the 1948 document reflects a high standard of quality and impact that Brookings scholars strive for to this day.*

80th Congress }
2d Session }
COMMITTEE PRINT

ADMINISTRATION OF UNITED STATES AID FOR A EUROPEAN RECOVERY PROGRAM

REPORT

TO THE

COMMITTEE ON FOREIGN RELATIONS UNITED STATES SENATE

ON

ADMINISTRATION OF UNITED STATES AID FOR
A EUROPEAN RECOVERY PROGRAM

Submitted at the request of the Chairman of the Committee
by
THE BROOKINGS INSTITUTION
January 22, 1948

Printed for the use of the Committee on Foreign Relations

UNITED STATES
GOVERNMENT PRINTING OFFICE
WASHINGTON : 1948

70852

COMMITTEE ON FOREIGN RELATIONS

ARTHUR H. VANDENBERG, Michigan, *Chairman*

ARTHUR CAPPER, Kansas

WALLACE H. WHITE, Jr. Maine

ALEXANDER WILEY, Wisconsin

H. ALEXANDER SMITH, New Jersey

BOURKE B. HICKENLOOPER, Iowa

HENRY CABOT LODGE, JR., Massachusetts

TOM CONNALLY, Texas

WALTER F. GEORGE, Georgia

ROBERT F. WAGNER, New York

ELBERT D. THOMAS, Utah

ALBEN W. BARKLEY, Kentucky

CARL A. HATCH, New Mexico

FRANCIS O. WILCOX, *Chief of Staff*

C.C. O'DAY, *Clerk*

INTRODUCTORY NOTE

Even before the Committee on Foreign Relations began its study of the European recovery program it was apparent that the major problems involved in the administration of such a program deserved very careful consideration. Accordingly, on December 30, 1947, the chairman of the committee requested the Brookings Institution to prepare a brief analysis of the main administrative proposals that have been put forward, taking into account the experience of our Government with respect to similar programs during recent years. It was believed that as a result of such a study certain basic principles might emerge which would be of assistance to the committee in its attempt to find the type of administrative organization that would help insure an effective ERP.

The report of the Brookings Institution is printed herewith for the use of the Senate and Committee on Foreign Relations. The conclusions of the Brookings Institution will be found on pages [64] to [76].

REPORT ON ADMINISTRATION OF
UNITED STATES AID FOR A
EUROPEAN RECOVERY PROGRAM

INTRODUCTION

This report on the administration of United States aid for a European recovery program has been prepared at the request of the chairman of the Committee on Foreign Relations of the United States Senate. In his request, the chairman asked the Brookings Institution to undertake a rapid review and analysis of the principal proposals that have been made for the administration of the program, taking into account the experience with the administration of similar programs during the past few years. Upon the basis of this study, an independent appraisal was requested of the requirements for an administrative organization that would insure maximum business efficiency in proper coordination with other aspects of our foreign policy and the conduct of foreign relations.

In this undertaking, a review has been made of the three major proposal emanating from within the Government, namely the report by the President's Committee on Foreign Aid (known as the Harriman committee); the reports of the House Select Committee on Foreign Aid (known as the Herter committee) and the bill, H.R. 4579 (the Herter bill), that embodies the recommendations of the committee; and the special message from the President to the Congress on December 19, 1947, together with the draft bill (subsequently introduced as H.R. 4840) and the supporting report submitted by the Department of State. Extensive consultations were held with many persons who participated in the preparation of the foregoing proposals and consideration was given to the bases upon which their conclusions were drawn.

Account has also been taken of the proposals for administration of the program that have been put forward by private organizations, such as the Chamber of Commerce of the United States, the National

Association of Manufacturers, the National Foreign Trade Council, the Congress of Industrial Organizations, and the National Planning Association—to name only a few—and of proposals and suggestions of a more informal nature made by private individuals both inside and outside the Government. Finally, recent American programs for overseas relief, economic development, and aid were reviewed by members of our staff who have had extensive experience in this general field.

The results of this study and the conclusions reached are presented in the three parts of this report. Part 1 outlines briefly the nature of the administrative problems involved in the proposed European Recovery Program. The outstanding issues that the Congress faces in determining the character of the administrative arrangements for the program are set forth in part 2, together with a summary of the main arguments that have been advanced with respect to each issue. Part 3 states the conclusions reached.

PART I
THE NATURE OF THE PROBLEM

The administration of United States aid for a European recovery program, in its manifold policy and operating aspects, must be considered in relation to the basic objectives of the program. The central purpose is to help the participating countries, individually and as a group, to help themselves in achieving economic stability and in strengthening free institutions. The attainment of this purpose requires the operation of a gigantic foreign economic program, which, in some of its phases, partakes of the character of business enterprise. But the administration of the program is not merely a business matter. In the nature of the case, the program involves relations among sovereign nations and is, therefore, inextricably bound up with a wide range of United States foreign policies at the highest level of government.

Once Congress approves the program, bilateral agreements must be negotiated by the United States Government with each participating European country, under which the latter will be required to accept certain obligations, varying according to circumstances, as a condition of receiving aid. Simultaneously, some arrangements will have to be worked out with the overall continuing organization that it is expected will be created in Europe by multilateral agreement among the participating countries. From time to time there will be need for subsequent negotiations involving possible modifications *of* these basic agreements. The program thus calls for the initial establishment and possible later revision of a new set of relationships among a large number of governments. It also calls for special liaison with a number of existing and contemplated international organizations, both European and general, in addition to the special organization set up by the participating countries.

The day-to-day administrative operations of the program will take place within the framework provided by this complex of agreements. The supplying of the goods and services under these agreements cannot be handled simply by turning an experienced purchasing agent loose with the requisite funds. A program must first be planned—in relation to the specific needs of each of the participating countries and with due regard to available supplies in the United States, as well as to the possibility of obtaining some portion of the materials from other countries. There is thus required wide knowledge of economic conditions in Europe, the capacity of the domestic economy, possibilities international trade, and negotiations with foreign governments as well as skill in routine business operations.

Since one of the objectives of the program is to promote rather than retard the resumption of commercial operations between countries, much of the procurement is expected to be carried on through normal business channels. Such purchases will, however, have to be guided by the administration to insure conformity with the program. Export controls, priorities, and powers of allocation will doubtless be required in some cases to lessen the adverse effect on the domestic economy. Provision will have to be made for the efficient use of transport facilities within in the United States and in overseas shipments. The employment of overseas transportation raises such questions of policy as the distribution of cargoes between United States and foreign-flag vessels, those concerning the sale or charter of United States Government-owned ships, the interests of the United States merchant marine and national defense, and problems of coordination in procurement and operation of shipping. Important decisions will also need to be made on a wide range of financial problems, relating both the expenditure of Government funds and to the stimulation of private financing.

Many of these activities will have a direct bearing on the capacity, health, and strength of the American economy and, from this standpoint, they are obviously not exclusively the concern of the administration of the European recovery program. In some cases the direct assistance of many departments of the Government will be necessary. The decisions to be made affect the policies not only of the Department of State, but also in some instances the Departments of the Treasury, Commerce, and Agriculture, the Military Establishment, the Maritime Commission, and other agencies of the Government.

At the European end, the administrative problems are of the most diverse character. The administration will be concerned, in every participating country, with such problems as the following: The adequacy of recovery programs; methods of allocating, distributing, and using American supplies; trends in export and import trade, including trade with nonparticipant European countries; currency reform and exchange stabilization; fiscal policies; the use and control of local currencies deposited in earmarked or special accounts; and facilitating the sale of special materials to the United States of stock piling and other purposes. In connection with joint undertakings that transcend the efforts of particular countries, the administration will need to collaborate closely with the organization established for that purpose by the participating countries.

To prevent the possibility of dissipating or misusing the aid given, it is vitally important that the administration set up certain tests by which to gauge the general progress of the program as a whole and the degree of compliance on the part of the European countries individually and collectively. Such tests must be worked out with responsible officials of the European governments. Because of constantly changing conditions the administration will need to have discretion within the framework of the commitments made in the government agreements. It is obvious that such decisions have an important bearing on many aspects of American foreign policy, especially if occasions arise for the termination of aid.

Western Germany will present many special problems, whether American economic operations there are integrated with the program worked out for the 16 European countries or merely coordinated with it. The situation in Germany differs, however, from that in the other because there is no sovereign German government with which to deal, and direct operations are therefore involved. These operations are complicated by the fact that they need to be coordinated with the operations of the other two occupying powers, Great Britain and France.

Two things are evident from this brief outline of the nature of the program: First, the administrative task is one of extraordinary magnitude and complexity, requiring an unusual combination of experience, skill, and judgment; and second, it is neither a purely business job nor a purely governmental operation, but a mixture of both. The problem before the Congress is thus to create administrative machinery that will insure an effective carrying out of the business aspects of the program in proper coordination with the requirements of our domestic economy and at the same time promote to the fullest possible extent the attainment of the Nation's foreign policy objectives.

PART 2
OUTSTANDING ISSUES

The major issues that the Congress faces in determining the character of the administrative arrangements for the European recovery program arise both from differences in evaluations of tasks to be performed and from varying interpretations of the results of the administrative experience of the Government, especially during and since the war, in administering similar programs

Despite these differences, current proposals for administering the program seem to be in agreement on the following points:

1. *A new agency.*—Primary responsibility for administering the program should be lodged in a new temporary administrative agency. Success of the program is so important to the national well-being of the United States that the organizational arrangement for the agency should be designed to attract men of outstanding ability to the Government for service in it.

2. *The need for flexibility.*—The unpredictable situations that may have to be faced and the speed that is necessary in carrying out the program if it is to be effective require that a large degree of financial and administrative flexibility should be inherent in any organization that is established.

3. *Organization abroad.*—The operations required in Europe are of such primary importance that an overseas organization will be essential.

Beyond these areas of agreement, however, lie many issues that must be resolved in prescribing the administrative arrangements for the program. Some of these must be determined by the Congress. Others may be left for later administrative determination, provided that the Congress lays down the guiding principles. The issues outlined in this section do not comprise all of the many issues that must be faced. But they appear to be of key importance in determining the character of the administrative arrangements that should be established.

To clarify the problem and sharpen the discussion the main alternatives that have been proposed for the solution of these outstanding issues are presented below. For purposes of discussion, the issues are grouped into three broad categories:

(1) Those relating to the status of the Government of the new agency, especially its relationship to the Department of State, and the organizational form and structure of the agency;

(2) Those involved in the assignment of administrative responsibilities for the execution of the program; and

(3) Those covering the form and responsibilities of the overseas organization for the program.

Conclusions with respect to these various issues are reserved for part 3 of this report.

I. STATUS AND FORM OF THE NEW AGENCY

Although there is general agreement that the Congress should establish a single agency that would be primarily responsible for administering United States aid for a European recovery program, there are wide differences of opinion on two points: (1) The status in the Government to be given the new agency; and (2) its organizational form and structure.

1. Status of the new agency

There are varying opinions on the degree of autonomy to be given the new agency, and these are reflected in current proposals. At the core of this issue is the perplexing and important question of the relation between the new agency and the Department of State. There appear to be four main alternatives:

(1) A new agency within the Department of State, internally autonomous but directly subject to the authority of the Secretary of State, and the head of it ranking with, but after, the Under Secretary of State;

(2) An agency separate from the Department of State but subject to the direction and control of the Secretary of State in all matters affecting the conduct of foreign policy;

(3) A "separate" agency in the executive branch of the Government subject only to the direction and control of the President in his role as the Chief Executive; and

(4) An "independent" agency, independent in the sense that it would be largely free from the control of the Chief Executive, as is the case with many of the Government corporations and of the independent agencies and commissions that perform regulatory or quasi-judicial functions.

Creation of an internally autonomous agency within the Department of State and directly subject to the authority of the Secretary of State would, it is argued, clarify once and for all the relation of the head of the new agency to the Secretary of State and in this manner would insure unified action in foreign policy and fix accountability both to the President and to the Congress. Against this it is argued that the proposal would impose on the Secretary of State responsibilities for procurement, allocation, and delivery of goods and services that would inject him into domestic agricultural, industrial, and financial problems extending far beyond the usual responsibilities of the Department of State.

The alternative of separating the agency from the Department of State and subjecting it to the direction and control of the Secretary of State only in matters affecting the conduct of foreign policy would, it is claimed, concentrate in the new agency all the functions relating to domestic and foreign operations of procurement and delivery that are of a business nature, and leave only the foreign-policy aspects of the program, subject to control by the Secretary of State. On the other hand, it is argued that the division of authority under this proposal would inevitably lead to administrative conflicts between the head of the new agency and the Secretary of State, which the President ultimately would have to settle in his role both as the Chief Executive and as the official charged by the Constitution with the conduct of the foreign relations of the United States.

The creation of a separate agency in the executive branch of the Government subject only to the direction and control of the President would have the great advantages, it is claimed, both of insuring centralization of responsibility and unity of administration and of giving ultimate authority to the President in his constitutional role of responsibility for the conduct of the United States foreign relations. Against this it is argued that this proposal would lead to greater administrative conflicts than in the previous alternative, since the legislative division of responsibility would be greater with the consequent risk of impairing the prestige and authority of the Secretary of State as the usual spokesman for the United States in foreign-policy matters. One current proposal seeks to meet this argument by making the Secretary of State a member of the advisory board to the head of the new agency, the board having the power "to establish and adjust general policies" for the agency.

Another argument made against the proposal for a

separate agency subject to Presidential control is that such an agency would be more susceptible to "politics" in its administrative operations. Establishment of an "independent" agency would, it is claimed, overcome this difficulty by placing the agency in the position of being able to perform its functions in a nonpartisan fashion and thus to eliminate any suspicion of "politics" in its operations. The counterargument, however, is that it might in effect remove from Presidential control an important part of his constitutional responsibility for the conduct of the foreign relations of the United States. A current proposal for an "independent" agency would meet this objection by requiring the "establishment" by the President of the "programs of United States aid to foreign countries, and policies in connection therewith" that the agency would have to follow.

2. *Organizational form and structure*

The issue of what form and structure to give the new agency has two principal aspects:

(1) The choice between a corporate or a noncorporate form of organization; and

(2) The choice between direction by a single administrator or by a board or commission.

These two questions are dealt with here independently of each other, because there appears to be nothing inherent in the corporate form of organization to require a board instead of a single administrator to head the new agency. In fact, one current proposal is for a corporation headed by an administrator. Similarly there appears to be nothing inherent in the noncorporate form to require a single administrator instead of a board.

The principal advantages claimed for the corporate form of organization are twofold: First, that it would have great financial and administrative flexibility because it would be free from the normal Government regulations relating to procurement, personnel, and auditing; and second, that it would be more "business-like" because it could enter into contracts, sue and be sued, settle claims in its own name, and in general use ordinary business financial controls and practices in a program that is essentially of a business character. Against this it is argued that the administrative and financial flexibility of a corporate form may be obtained in the noncorporate form by giving the new agency the necessary exemption from the provisions of law normally governing procurement, personnel, and auditing. It is argued further that the business analogy should not be pushed too far because that would be placing undue emphasis on the business features at the expense of the forcing policy and other governmental features of the program.

Regardless of whether the new agency was of the corporate or noncorporate form, it is claimed that with a single administrator at the head of it the centralization of control and responsibility for operations under the European recovery program would be assured and the rapid administrative decisions that will be required could be made. But against this it is argued that too much power would be concentrated in one individual for the large financial outlays and for the basic policy decisions that will be required under the program.

To deal with this latter point, it has been proposed that the Congress should create an advisory board to the administrator with power to establish and adjust general policies, but with the clear understanding that the operating decisions should be made by the head of the new agency. Two separate arguments, however, are made against this proposal. First, it is claimed that Congress should not establish such a body by law but that if experience indicates that the administrator would benefit from the advice of a consultative body it could be established at any time by Executive order. Second, it is argued that an advisory board is not enough and that the control of the operations should be vested in a bipartisan or nonpartisan board of private persons, possessing the necessary business experience, judgment, and managerial capacity to achieve the maximum benefits of which the program is capable. This would assure, it is claimed, broad representation in the determination of the policies and operations of the new agency and thus would assist in maintaining public confidence that the program was being carried out in the best interests of the country as a whole. Against this second type of argument, it is claimed experience has shown that the board type of organization is unwieldy, which militates against rapid operating decisions and flexibility in administration. Public confidence in the operations of the new agency could be instilled, it is argued, by the creation of an advisory group consisting of representatives of the public, business, agriculture, and labor, on lines similar to the group in the Office of War Mobilization and Reconversion.

II. RESPONSIBILITY FOR THE EXECUTION OF THE PROGRAM

The issues arising out of the assignment of general responsibilities for the execution of the program center around seven principal points. First there is the question of the administrative determination of broad programs and general operating policies, all within the framework of the overall limitations on European aid prescribed the Congress. Closely related to this are two other issues: The negotiation of agreements with foreign governments; and the control of the funds that are made available for the program. Next are four issues directly connected with facilitating the procurement and delivery of United States aid; determination of the methods of financing; the manner in which the services and facilities of existing Federal agencies are to be utilized; the administration of export controls; and what responsibilities, if any, the new agency is to have in relation to other foreign-aid programs undertaken with United States funds.

All these issues must be viewed in the light of the generally agreed opinion that financial and administrative flexibility must prevail in the execution of the program.

1. Broad programs and general policies

Important problems arise because requirements for United States aid under the European recovery program must be fitted in with United States exports to other parts of the world. Existing agencies of the Government, especially the Departments of the Treasury, Commerce, Agriculture, Interior, Labor, the National Military Establishment, and the Maritime Commission are concerned with the impact on the American economy of foreign requirements for United States exports. Some of these departments, in addition to the Department of State, also have an interest in the foreign aspects of the problems, and the overall decisions of national policy that concern several departments may ultimately require Presidential decision.

This issue has three principal features: (a) The agency that should, in the first instance, be responsible for initiating and sponsoring programs and operating policies for European aid; (b) the extent of the participation of other Federal agencies in the formulating process; (c) the mechanism needed to insure coordination of European aid with other domestic and foreign policies of the United States before final approval is given.

There are two main proposals for the agency that is to initiate and sponsor the program and policies: The new agency that would be established to administer the program; or another agency, often suggested as being one that would be part of the office of the President. Proponents of the plan for using the new agency for this purpose argue that unless the agency principally responsible for administering the aid is also responsible for initiating programs and policies for it, administrative confusion is sure to result. Those who favor using a small, central planning agency claim that the problem is larger than developing programs and policies for European aid, and that an overall agency would maintain the impartiality that is required.

It is implicit in all the major proposals that while primary responsibility for initiating and sponsoring programs and policies should rest with one agency, the latter would have to establish relations at the working level with other agencies concerned. The advantages of establishing these interconnections are obvious. Any counterargument would have to rest on the assumption that the single agency could take sole responsibility for all economic activity in the foreign and domestic fields, including even the determination of the availability of commodities for consumption in the United States. None of the current proposals has gone as far as this. The crux of the administrative problem, however, is to determine the mechanism for giving weight to the views of the different agencies, and for resolving conflicts between them, in establishing the programs and policies for European aid. On the one hand it is argued that the authorizing legislation should prescribe this mechanism in detail and clearly fix responsibilities and procedures. Against this it is argued that to do so would reduce administrative flexibility, especially since most of the current proposals assume that the President as Chief Executive would be responsible in the final analysis for resolving conflicts among the agencies. Therefore, he should, it is claimed, be given the freedom to establish such new procedures as he may deem necessary, or to continue those now in existence.

2. Negotiation of agreements with foreign countries

This issue depends largely on the relation that is to prevail between the new agency and the Department of State. It arises principally with respect to the basic and subsidiary agreements with participating European governments, but to some extent it also affects negotiations that may be required with non-European governments concerning the procurement and financing of "offshore" assistance. There appear to be three possible solutions. Primary responsibility for negotiating the agreements might be lodged by legislation in (a) the new agency, (b) the Department of State, or (c) the President.

No proposal so far made lodges complete responsibility in the new agency, and the arguments deal with the degree in which the President or other agencies should participate. The proponents of placing maximum responsibility with the new agency argue that it is necessary to fix responsibility for these negotiations where, from the practical point of view, they belong, namely, in the agency charged with the successful operation of the program. The main counterargument is that this would remove the primary responsibility from the place where it constitutionally belongs, namely, with the President or, by his delegation, with the Secretary of State.

To justify placing responsibility with the Secretary of State the further arguments are added that this is necessary to avoid the risk of having two foreign policies, and that only the basic agreements are to be negotiated by the Department of State in consultation with the new agency, the latter being free to negotiate subsequent subsidiary agreements in consultation with other appropriate agencies.

Finally, the argument is advanced for placing the responsibility with the President on the ground that from the constitutional standpoint that is where it legally belongs. On the other hand, it is pointed out that since the President will in practice delegate this authority to the Secretary of State or some other officer of the Government, this fact should be recognized in framing legislation.

3. Control of the funds

Administrative control of the funds that will be appropriated for European aid is especially important from the standpoint of determining the overall programs and policies to be followed. The alternatives that have been proposed are to vest control in (a) the new agency, and (b) the President.

The argument advanced for vesting control of the funds in the new agency, through direct appropriation to it, is that centralization of responsibility and accountability for the operations of the program would be increased. Against this it is argued that the control of the funds should lie with the President through direct appropriation to him because otherwise expenditure might be made in a manner detrimental to United States foreign relations or too late adequately to further them. In the latter possibility, the question would arise whether the new agency, if given exclusive control, would at any time be invading the constitutional prerogatives of the Present.

4. Determination of methods of financing

The fundamental question under this issue refers to the choice between the alternatives of (a) strict congressional control through legislative definition of new methods to be used, and (b) leaving discretion to the new agency in the interest of administrative flexibility.

It is argued that there should be a clear delimitation of functions between the new agency and the Export-Import Bank, and that the responsibilities of each under the European-aid program could be fixed by legislation. Current proposals would give to the new agency the primary function of administering only that part of the aid program, consisting principally of food, fuels, and fertilizer, that must be, for the most part, provided in the form of grants, and would assign to the Export-Import Bank the responsibility for all loans covering commodities to be processed and certain types of specialized equipment. This would be done on the assumption that the International Bank would provide the necessary loans for capital expansion. It is claimed that in this way confusion would be avoided that might result from granting in the form of loans advances that are in reality grants, and that a careful and rigid distinction between the two would encourage the flow of private investment by eliminating from the obligations of the recipient countries debts that had not been incurred with any genuine expectation of repayment.

On the other hand, the main argument advanced for leaving discretion to the agency in this important matter is that the program as it develops will change considerably the needs for financing particular com-modities to particular destinations. An attempt to define beforehand methods of financing by types of assistance would prevent the new administration from varying the methods in accordance with the changing circumstances in the recipient countries affecting their ability to make payment. It is also argued that, within the loan category of assistance, there is need of con-siderable flexibility with a view to taking advantage of all opportunities to enlist private capital, including the financing of raw materials and equipment necessary to expand the operation of existing European productive facilities. Furthermore, it is pointed out that in the absence of legislative definition of methods of financ-ing, the Congress would still retain a general control over developing the program because of the necessity of making annual appropriations. Finally, it is claimed that discretion and flexibility in the administration of the aid could be combined with legislative direction to consult with the National Advisory Council and to make use of existing agencies, for the purpose of integrating the financial operations of the program with the established mechanisms for determining the overall international monetary and investment policy of the United States.

5. *Utilization of existing Federal agencies*
Existing agencies are already performing important functions of the type involved in the procurement

and delivery of aid to Europe, especially the Departments of the Treasury, Agriculture, Interior, Commerce, Army, the Office of Defense Transportation, and the Interstate Commerce Commission. The alternatives are (a) to make the most of these existing agencies, or (b) to combine all the necessary functions in the new agency.

The argument advanced for using, the greatest extent practicable, existing machinery as it stands is that to transfer staffs and functions from existing agencies to the new agency would not only require drastic changes in the permanent administrative departments for a purpose that is only temporary, but would also seriously affect the efficiency of operations geared, as they currently are, to the framework and coordinated operations of their respective agencies. On the other hand, it is argued that unless these operations were to be utilized by transferring them to the immediate direction and control of the new agency, there would be not only extensive duplication between the staff and operations of the new agency and those of existing agencies to the detriment of the program, but also the risk of too great a diffusion of operating decisions. To meet this latter point, it is claimed that machinery could be created for the centralization and coordination of decisions. And the further claim is made that in respect to some functions, especially the direction of overseas shipping, such machinery will have to be created regardless of whether the functions are allowed to remain in existing agencies or are transferred to the new agency.

6. Administration of export controls

Special importance attaches to this issue because of the world-wide range of United States exports. The alternatives proposed are: (a) to retain the present arrangements; and (b) to transfer the administration of the controls to the new agency.

The argument advanced for retaining the operation of export controls in the Department of Commerce, in consultation with the new agency and other agencies concerned, is that a balance must be struck between the total needs of European countries, which the new agency will present, and the needs of the United States and the rest of the world, which other agencies will present. In the event of a dispute between the new agency and the Department of Commerce or other agencies, the settlement of it would, as in other cases, require appeal to the President as Chief Executive. It is pointed out that it would be a disadvantage, if, by centralizing powers over export controls in the new agency, the latter was compelled to act as both advocate and judge in passing on European claims.

Those who favor placing in the new agency all responsibility for administering export controls base their argument primarily on the claim that administration of these controls on an overall basis by a second agency would handicap the rapid and efficient administration of the European recovery program by the new agency, since the greatest need for the use of export controls would arise from the requirements of the aid program.

7. *Administration of other aid programs*

It is generally assumed that the interim-aid program now being administered by the Department of State will be transferred to the new agency. Two other major problems remain, however: The responsibility of the new agency for administering economic re-habilitation and reconstruction of western Germany in the European recovery program, and for all other foreign-aid programs, including such programs as Greek-Turkish aid and possible future programs of greater aid to such areas as China and Latin Amer-ica. The alternatives are (a) to concentrate operations similar to or connected with those to be performed in the European program in the new agency or (b) to disperse the operations among other agencies.

Germany presents an issue of immediate and crit-ical importance because of its central position in the European economic system. At present the Depart-ment of the Army is the responsible operating agency, although it has been suggested that a civil adminis-tration may soon supersede the Army in some of its functions. Whatever step is taken in this direction, the Army will still be responsible in some respects as the occupation authority, and the need will arise for coordination of activities.

The argument advanced for centering the relevant economic functions for Germany in the new agency is that it would be best equipped to deal, as part of the overall program, with the complicated economic problems of German reconstruction. Against adopting this course it is argued that the political and military aspects of the German problems are so intertwined with the economic that it would be disadvantageous to make the new agency mainly responsible for the economic functions. It is claimed, however, that provided there was proper consultation with the Department of State and Army, the new agency might well make requests to the Congress for aid to Germany as part of its overall program.

It is pointed out that the advantage of consolidating the administration of all other programs of foreign aid, regardless of type, in the new agency is that it would avoid the difficulties experienced during and after the war from the dispersal of programs among agencies. On the other hand, programs such as the current aid to Greece and Turkey have certain military features which, it is argued, make it impossible to administer them on the more businesslike basis contemplated for the European-aid program. In the case of possible future aid to Latin America, for example, it is argued that these military features might not be present so strongly, and that great advantages from the point of view of general programing and policy as well as operations would be derived from combining such future aid with the European program in a single agency.

III. FORM AND RESPONSIBILITIES OF THE OVERSEAS ORGANIZATION

Although there is general agreement that an overseas organization will be required in connection with the European recovery program, two major points are at issue: (1) The form of the organization in individual countries; and (2) the status and responsibilities of the chief representative for the program in Europe. Both of these, in turn, reflect the basic issues on the status of the new agency in the United States, especially its relation to the Department of State.

1. Form of the organization in individual countries

There is agreement that special representatives with appropriate staff will be required to administer the operations in each European country participating in the program. If the decision is made at the one extreme, however, that the new agency in the United States should be separate in status from the Department of State, the question of whether there should be a separate overseas organization will be raised in its most acute form. On the other hand, if the decision is made at the other extreme, that the new agency should be wholly within the framework of the Department of State, the question may not appear so pressing. On the assumption that the new agency in the United States is separate in status from the Department of Sate, the form of the overseas organization would in large measure be determined by five decisions on subsidiary issues: (1) Procedures to be used for recruiting and appointing overseas personnel and the pay and allowances to be given them; (2) the line of responsibility between the new agency and the representatives overseas for the program; (3) whether the representatives overseas for the program should constitute a separate mission or be consolidated with existing United States diplomatic missions; (4) control over communications between the new agency and the overseas representatives for the program; and (5) the control, if any, to be exerted by the United States ambassadors over the negotiations undertaken between the overseas representatives for the program and the governments of foreign countries.

In order to attract qualified personnel from the business world for the overseas operations, it is claimed that the head of the new agency should be free to engage a staff with the necessary qualifications without being unduly restricted by regulations governing appointments and pay of Foreign Service reserve officers. On the other side it is argued that to use such recruitment and appointment procedures without regard to those used by the Department of State and to provide greater pay and privileges for the special personnel than the Foreign Service officers are now receiving would be disruptive of, and demoralizing to, the existing staffs of American missions abroad.

Special representatives for the program in the individual countries could report either directly to the head of the new agency or to him through the ambassador or the Department of State. Unity of authority and administration demands, it is argued, that the special representatives should report to the head of the new agency. On the other hand, it is argued that unless these representatives reported through the ambassador, there would be bound to be a lack of coordination and even conflicts between the ambassador and the special representatives, to the detriment of United States interests and objectives.

The argument in favor of maintaining a special mission for the program in each country is that the organization must preserve its own identity for efficiency in fitting its work in individual countries into the network of operations under the program. But it is also pointed out on the other side that if this mission were consolidated with the embassies, certain advantages would be obtained from closer relations between the staffs and from the joint use of services and facilities. A middle ground between the two has been suggested in providing that the head of the new agency organization in each individual country, even if the organization is a separate mission, should have direct access to the ambassador as an essential requirement in duplicating in the field the safeguards that would be established in the United States to protect foreign policy objectives. The ambassador on his part should be informed of all activities of the mission.

An acute question is raised, however, regarding the control of communications between the representatives in the field and the new agency in the United States. On the one hand, communications between the two could take place without any provision that the ambassador or the Department of State be informed. On the other hand, all such communications could be subject to the complete control of the ambassador and the Department of State. Again a middle ground that has been suggested would be that of the ambassador having access to all communications between the special representative in Europe and the new agency in the United States. This procedure would not, as is claimed, prevent these representatives from communicating directly with the head of the new agency but the ambassador would have the right to comment and, if necessary, register objections from the standpoint of foreign policy before action was taken.

Negotiations and discussions between the special representatives for the program and the foreign government is a problem similar to the above. It has been argued that such negotiations should not be subject to the control of the ambassador since operating problems would be for the most part involved. Against this, however, it is claimed that it is difficult to distinguish in such discussions and negotiations between policy and technical matters. A compromise between these two views has been suggested by giving to the representatives of the new agency the authority to conduct negotiations with representatives of a foreign government, while keeping the course of negotiations subject to comment and objection by the ambassador as the chief representative of the United States Government in that country.

2. *Status and responsibilities of the chief representative in Europe*

There appears to be general agreement that the chief representative should have ambassadorial rank and that he could be accredited to any continuing European organization for administering aid to Europe and possibly be the United States representative on the United Nations Economic Commission for Europe. The questions remain of the functions to be performed and whether the chief representative would be made responsible to the administrator of the new agency, to the President, or to the Secretary of State. The two questions are interrelated, but it is argued that whatever the line of responsibility, in the interest of flexibility of administration, the functions and responsibilities of the chief representative should not be too closely defined by legislative enactment. On the other side, it is argued that explicit legislative provisions should be made on these points because of the importance of the position and the heavy responsibilities that might be involved.

The principal point at issue in regard to the functions of the chief representative is the extent to which he will have the power to direct the operations of the special representatives for the program in the individual countries. It is argued that he should be given considerable power in this respect in order to provide a focal point of administrative authority in Europe. Against this the argument is made that it might cut across the lines of authority between the head of the new agency and the special representatives in individual countries as well as confuse the relations between the new agency and the Department of State. It is claimed that in view of the inherent difficulty of deciding beforehand the relative merits of these alternatives, the functions of the chief representative should not be closely defined by legislation, but left to be worked out in the light of experience, although the necessity of giving him some coordinating function should be recognized.

Since the functions of the representative would in any event involve him in foreign policy questions at a high level, an argument has been advanced for making him responsible directly to the President. The counterargument in favor of making him responsible directly and finally to the head of a new agency is based on the belief that this would contribute to maximum unity in the administration of the program, both in the United States and abroad.

PART 3
CONCLUSIONS

An examination of the issues involved in the establishment of an effective organization for the administration of the European recovery program, in the light of an appraisal of the complex nature of the problem and of the lessons of recent experience, leads us to the conclusions stated below. These conclusions relate to what in our judgment are the major requirements for such an organization and some of the main principals that should guide its establishment and operation. Attention is given only to those aspects of the problem which bear directly on the administrative arrangements for the European recovery program now under discussion.

1. Creation and status of a new agency

The magnitude and special character of the task to be performed require the creation of a new and separate operating agency. The activities involved in carrying out the program will constitute an important segment of the larger area of the conduct of United States foreign relations, for which the President is responsible under the Constitution. These activities will have a heavy impact on the policies and operations of other departments and agencies that deal with domestic affairs under the direction of the Chief Executive. The new agency could function effectively, therefore, only if it were to be made an integral part of the executive branch of the Government.

To place the new agency in the Department of State would impose upon the Secretary of State responsibility for a wide range of activities in the economic and business field. However, because of the responsibilities lodged in the Department of State with respect to the formulation and execution of foreign policies, it is essential that its position be adequately safeguarded.

Hence, a new and separate agency should be created in the executive branch of the Government to serve as the focal point of the administration of the program. It should function through effective working relations with the Department of State and the other agencies of the Government which are described below.

2. A single administrator of Cabinet status

Experience has demonstrated that in an operation of such magnitude, requiring speed of decision and centralization of responsibility for policy, a single administrator is more satisfactory than a board or a committee.

For an effective performance of his functions, the administrator will need to be given a status that will put him on a footing of equality with the heads of other agencies and departments of the Government with which it will be necessary for him to develop effective working relationships. No system of inter-agency coordination has yet been devised that can escape the necessity of final appeals to the President as the superior authority in the event of unreconciled differences between the heads of the agencies involved. It is essential, therefore, in this case to make sure that the administrator will have as direct access to the President as the heads of the other agencies with which he will need to coordinate his activities.

> Hence, the responsibilities assigned to the new agency and the powers given to it should be vested in a single administrator who should be appointed by the President, with the advice and consent of the Senate, and who should serve at the President's pleasure. The rank of the administrator should be the equivalent of Cabinet officer, and he should be responsible only to the President.

3. Form of the agency

The form of the new agency must be such as to provide sufficient flexibility of structure and operation and to attract outstanding personnel. If the Congress makes the necessary authorization for exemption from existing regulations, this is possible whether the form of the agency is corporate or noncorporate. On balance, the noncorporate form would appear to be more in keeping with the suggested position of the new agency in the executive branch of the Government on a plane with Cabinet departments.

Hence, the new agency should have a noncorporate form, but the administrator should be exempted from existing limitations on salaries for a limited number of his personnel; on per diem compensation and travel allowances; and, as necessary, on making contracts and on the expenditure of Government funds. The administrator should maintain an adequate system of accounting and control, subject to post-audit by the General Accounting Office in accordance with commercial practices.

4. *Advisory bodies and publicity*

Because of the range of problems involved and the far-reaching consequences of the programs, public confidence in the undertaking will be increased if provision is made for the administrator to have the benefit, through consultation and advice, of the knowledge and experience of private citizens. For the same reason, the fullest practicable measure of publicity should be given to the operations under the program.

> Hence, there should be created an advisory committee or board, composed of eminent citizens of broad and varied experience, to be appointed by the President. It should be made clear that the committee or board should not be vested with administrative responsibility, but should only be advisory to the administrator, who should act as its chairman. The administrator should be authorized to set up special advisory bodies and to consult with representatives of industry, labor, agriculture, and with other private citizens. Periodic reports should be made by the President to the Congress concerning the activities under the program.

5. Relations with other agencies

In administering the program, it is important to avoid a split arrangement that would center authority for policy determination in one department or agency and vest responsibilities for execution in another agency. Experience has amply demonstrated the impracticability of achieving the necessary unity of direction and administration by that method. Such a concept of administration is essentially negative or at most permissive in that it sets many limitations but offers few directions for positive action. In this case, it is essential to place primary responsibility for the formulation of operating policies and programs clearly upon the official who also has the responsibility for seeing to their execution. Only by such concentration of responsibility can there be adequate coordination of the complex considerations involved and the strong sponsorship that will be necessary if the program requirements are to receive the full recognition which their merit warrants.

Hence, the administrator, subject to the overall authority of the President, should be responsible for formulating programs, determining financial and material requirements, and, in consultation with the departments and agencies concerned, insuring the fulfillment of those requirements.

In obtaining allocations of scarce materials and services, the administrator should proceed in consultation with the departments or agencies that are responsible for conserving supplies. The procedures or special arrangements required for interagency consultation and assistance in the allocation process should be prescribed from time to time by the President, in the light of experience. These procedures should cover both domestic allocations and foreign allocations, including commercial exports, and should be carried out within the framework of the existing arrangements for the administration of export and other controls involved in the execution of the program. In case agreement cannot be reached with respect to the allocation of scarce materials, the matter would of course have to be referred to the President.

The administrator should have the responsibility for determining what services of procurement, storage, transportation, or other handling are necessary to insure delivery of supplies in conformity with approved programs, and should be responsible for working out arrangements for the effective performance of these services. Hence, he should determine when supplies are to be purchased through private trade facilities and when public procurement is necessary. He should have authority to enter into arrangements with other agencies for the utilization of their facilities or personnel in carrying out those functions, on such terms as may be mutually agreed upon, to prevent duplication of facilities, to insure efficient performance of the necessary procurement and handling series, and to protect his position as the official primarily responsible for execution of the program.

The control and allocation of funds, under the provisions of the legislation, should be the responsibility of the President.

The financial arrangements to be used should be the responsibility of the administrator, in consultation with the National Advisory Council on International Monetary and Financial Problems. If decision is made to permit the Export-Import

Bank to act as the administrator's agent in arranging loans to the participating countries, its authority should be accordingly amended.

The President should be given authority to transfer to the new agency the administration of any current programs involving United States foreign aid to participating countries. The question of whether the administration of any future foreign aid programs should be made the responsibility of the agency should be left for determination by the Congress as the occasion arises.

6. *The position of the Department of State*

Because of the responsibilities vested in the Department of State in connection with the conduct of foreign relations, the position of this Department in the administration of the European recovery program is obviously of paramount importance. The Department is vitally concerned with all operations under the program that may affect this country's foreign relations and policies. Occasions may arise in which a choice may need to be made between decisions under the program and more general foreign policy decisions. Arrangements, therefore, are necessary under which the administrator and the Secretary of State would so concert their respective activities as to strengthen and make more effective the conduct of the country's foreign relations.

Hence, while the President alone should be authorized to enter into formal agreements with foreign governments, within the scope prescribed by the legislation, and to determine the methods and procedures for the conduct of the negotiations involved, he should, in practice, charge the Secretary of State with responsibility, under this authority, for the conduct of negotiations for the conclusion of initial basic agreements and for subsequent modifications of them, with such participation by the administrator as the latter may, with the President's approval, deem necessary. Similarly, the President should charge the administrator with responsibility, under his authority, for the conduct of negotiations with foreign governments relative to operations under the program, with such participation by the Secretary of State as the latter may, with the approval of the President, deem necessary.

The administrator should keep the Secretary of State fully and currently informed on all actual or prospective activities of the new agency; and, conversely, the Secretary of State should keep the administrator fully and currently informed on pertinent departmental policies and developments. To this end effective working relations should be established between the new agency and the Department of State.

The Secretary of State should have the authority to request the administrator for information on any matters that in his judgment have an important bearing on the conduct of foreign policy. He should have the right to enter objections to any proposed action by the administrator, to make proposals to the administrator, and to call attention to the consequences of failure to act. In the case of objection to contemplated action, such action should be deferred until the differences of view are adjusted by consultation between the Secretary of State and the administrator, or by decision of the President. The same process of adjustment should apply to other differences of view.

7. Overseas organization in individual countries

In formulating, carrying out, and reviewing programs, representation in each of the participating countries will be required. Such representatives must have special competence for dealing with the many technical aspects of the recovery program. In their work they will necessarily be in intimate contact with many departments of the participant governments, and the head of the group will on occasion have to confer with the highest officials. There is need, therefore, for effective relations with the regular embassies and legations of the United States in these countries.

Hence, the special representatives for the program in each individual country should be organized into a special mission, the head of which should be made a member of the regular mission in that country and should have a rank second only to that of the chief of the regular mission in that country. The head of the special mission should be responsible to the administrator, but should keep the ambassador or minister currently and fully informed on all his activities, actual or contemplated. The chief of the regular diplomatic mission should have the right to enter objections to contemplated actions, to make proposals to the head of the special mission, and to call attention to the consequences of failure to act. In the case of objection to a contemplated action, the proposed action should be deferred pending reference of the matter to Washington for determination. The head of the special mission should be free to communicate directly with the administrator, with the heads of the other special missions, and with the special representative referred to below.

For the performance of his functions abroad, the administrator should have the authority to recruit the necessary personnel. The pay and allowances of the representatives for the program in individual countries should correspond to those of Foreign Service reserve officers who might be performing similar tasks, with the understanding that, in the event that is it impossible to obtain qualified personnel on these terms for certain of the necessary positions, the President should have the power to exempt these positions from existing limitations. The administrator should have the right, with the approval of the Secretary of State, to recruit personnel through the facilities of the Foreign Service, but should not be restricted solely to that method.

8. Representation in organizations in participating countries
The success of the whole European recovery program will depend in large measure upon the effective cooperation among the participating countries—which they have themselves pledged. To achieve this purpose it will be necessary for these countries to develop continuing organizations through which cooperative plans and projects can be made effective. Provision should therefore be made for representation of the United States in such organizations as may be established.

Hence, there should be appointed by the President, with the advice and consent of the Senate, a special representative of the United States Government with a rank equivalent to that of an ambassador. The functions of this official should relate primarily to matters which require joint negotiation with two or more participant countries and cannot therefor be handled through the representatives established in individual countries.

His instructions on such matters should be formulated in conformity with the general arrangements established in the United States for the administration of the program and its integration with the foreign policy of the United States. He should keep the administrator, the Secretary of State, and the heads of the embassies and legations concerned fully and currently informed of his activities. He should consult with the heads of the special missions and the chiefs of the regular missions, meet with them as necessary, and be entitled to receive their assistance.

THREE

ESSENTIALS TO PEACE

Marshall's Nobel Peace Prize Lecture

On December 10, 1953, George C. Marshall became the first professional soldier to receive the Nobel Peace Prize. However, it was Marshall's tenure as a diplomat on display as he received the prize for the European Recovery Program's economic revitalization of Europe. The Oslo ceremony was not without cold war drama; King Haakon VII led a standing ovation to overcome a wave of impromptu protest by pro-communist members of the audience. In Marshall's acceptance address the following day, the then retired general highlighted the "essentials of peace," the combination of military preparedness, sufficient economic opportunity, and adherence to democratic values that would keep the peace.

In this book's afterword, "Of Statecraft and War," Jones and Moreland seek to apply these notions to the contemporary period. Their work accords with the central theme of Marshall's address: the need to understand and draw on our history as we shape the present. As Marshall advised, we must "seek to understand the conditions . . . which have led to past tragedies and should strive to determine the great fundamentals which must govern a peaceful progression toward a constantly higher level of civilization."

ELEVENTH HOUR
MARCH 9, 1948

COURTESY OF THE GEORGE C. MARSHALL
FOUNDATION, LEXINGTON, VIRGINIA

I

I have been greatly and surprisingly honored in the past twenty-four hours, and in return I have been requested to speak here tonight. While no subject has been suggested, it is quite evident that the cause of peace is preeminent in your minds.

Discussions without end have been devoted to the subject of peace, and the efforts to obtain a general and lasting peace have been frequent through many years of world history. There has been success temporarily, but all have broken down, and with the most tragic consequences since 1914. What I would like to do is point our attention to some directions in which efforts to attain peace seem promising of success.

I will try to phrase my views or suggestions in the simplest possible terms though I lack the magic and artistry of that great orator whom the Nobel Committee in Stockholm so appropriately honored yesterday. In making my statement I will assume your familiarity with the discussions and efforts of the past eight years and also with something of the conditions

which have governed each long continued peace in world history.

I would like to make special mention of the years of the Pax Romana, which endured through almost all of the first two centuries of the Christian era. I do so because of a personal incident which made a profound impression on me in the spring of 1919. Arriving late at night in Chaumont, the American Headquarters in France, I sought shelter for the night in the house of a group of friends. I found they were temporarily absent; so I selected an unoccupied room and looked about for a book to read as I waited for sleep to come. The books available were mostly in French or German. Since I was unable to read them with facility, I looked further and finally found an English textbook on the history of Gaul. Casting about for an interesting portion, I landed on a description of the famous Roman Peace. Included in this description was a statement of the dispositions of the Roman troops during this prolonged period, a legion at Cologne, another at Coblenz, a third at Mayence, and the reserve at Trier. Now those happened to be the identical dispositions of our Allied Forces some eighteen hundred years later, with the Peace Commission sitting in Paris and evolving the policy of the League of Nations.

I would not wish to imply that the military deployment I have just described corresponds to the

protective NATO deployment of today. The threat today is quite different, but I do think that this remarkable historical repetition does suggest that we have walked blindly, ignoring the lessons of the past, with, in our century, the tragic consequences of two world wars and the Korean struggle as a result.

In my country my military associates frequently tell me that we Americans have learned our lesson. I completely disagree with this contention and point to the rapid disintegration between 1945 and 1950 of our once vast power for maintaining the peace. As a direct consequence, in my opinion, there resulted the brutal invasion of South Korea, which for a time threatened the complete defeat of our hastily arranged forces in that field. I speak of this with deep feeling because in 1939 and again in the early fall of 1950 it suddenly became my duty, my responsibility, to rebuild our national military strength in the very face of the gravest emergencies.

These opening remarks may lead you to assume that my suggestions for the advancement of world peace will rest largely on military strength. For the moment the maintenance of peace in the present hazardous world situation does depend in very large measure on military power, together with Allied cohesion. But the maintenance of large armies for an indefinite period is not a practical or a promising basis for policy. We must stand together strongly for these

present years, that is, in this present situation; but we must, I repeat, we must find another solution, and that is what I wish to discuss this evening.

There has been considerable comment over the awarding of the Nobel Peace Prize to a soldier. I am afraid this does not seem as remarkable to me as it quite evidently appears to others. I know a great deal of the horrors and tragedies of war. Today, as chairman of the American Battle Monuments Commission, it is my duty to supervise the construction and maintenance of military cemeteries in many countries overseas, particularly in Western Europe. The cost of war in human lives is constantly spread before me, written neatly in many ledgers whose columns are gravestones. I am deeply moved to find some means or method of avoiding another calamity of war. Almost daily I hear from the wives, or mothers, or families of the fallen. The tragedy of the aftermath is almost constantly before me.

I share with you an active concern for some practical method for avoiding war. Let me first say that I regard the present highly dangerous situation as a very special one, which naturally dominates our thinking on the subject of peace, but which should not, in my opinion, be made the principal basis for our reasoning towards the manner for securing a condition of long continued peace. A very strong military posture is vitally necessary today. How long it must continue I am not prepared to estimate, but I am sure that it is too

narrow a basis on which to build a dependable, long-enduring peace. The guarantee for a long continued peace will depend on other factors in addition to a moderated military strength, and no less important. Perhaps the most important single factor will be a spiritual regeneration to develop goodwill, faith, and understanding among nations. Economic factors will undoubtedly play an important part. Agreements to secure a balance of power, however disagreeable they may seem, must likewise be considered. And with all these there must be wisdom and the will to act on that wisdom.

II

In this brief discussion, I can give only a very limited treatment of these great essentials to peace. However, I would like to select three more specific areas for closer attention.

The *first* relates to the possibilities of better education in the various factors affecting the life of peaceful security, both in terms of its development and of its disruption. Because wisdom in action in our Western democracies rests squarely upon public understanding, I have long believed that our schools have a key role to play. Peace could, I believe, be advanced through careful study of all the factors which have gone into the various incidents now historical that have marked the breakdown of peace in the past.

As an initial procedure our schools, at least our colleges but preferably our senior high schools, as we call them, should have courses which not merely instruct our budding citizens in the historical sequence of events of the past, but which treat with almost scientific accuracy the circumstances which have marked the breakdown of peace and have led to the disruption of life and the horrors of war.

There may perhaps have been a "last clear chance" to avoid the tragic conflagrations of our century. In the case of World War II, for example, the challenge may well have come in the early thirties, and passed largely unrecognized until the situation was unlikely to be retrieved. We are familiar with specific events such as the march into the Rhineland or aggression in Ethiopia or Manchuria. Perhaps there was also a last clear chance to begin to build up the strength of the democracies to keep the military situation in equilibrium. There may also have been a last clear chance to penetrate to the spirit of the peoples of the nations threatening the peace, and to find ways of peaceful adjustment in the economic field as well. Certainly, had the outcome of the war, with its devastation and disruption, been foreseen, and had there been an understanding on all sides of the problems that were threatening the peace, I feel sure that many possibilities for accommodation would have been much more thoroughly explored.

It is for this reason that I believe our students must

first seek to understand the conditions, as far as possible without national prejudices, which have led to past tragedies and should strive to determine the great fundamentals which must govern a peaceful progression toward a constantly higher level of civilization. There are innumerable instructive lessons out of the past, but all too frequently their presentation is highly colored or distorted in the effort to present a favorable national point of view. In our school histories at home, certainly in years past, those written in the North present a strikingly different picture of our Civil War from those written in the South. In some portions it is hard to realize they are dealing with the same war. Such reactions are all too common in matters of peace and security. But we are told that we live in a highly scientific age. Now the progress of science depends on facts and not fancies or prejudice. Maybe in this age we can find a way of facing the facts and discounting the distorted records of the past.

I am certain that a solution of the general problem of peace must rest on broad and basic understanding on the part of its peoples. Great single endeavors like a League of Nations, a United Nations, and undertakings of that character, are of great importance and in fact absolutely necessary, but they must be treated as steps toward the desired end.

We must depend in large measure on the impartiality of those who teach. Their approach must be on a scientific basis in order to present the true facts.

The scientists, no matter of what nationality, make a common approach to their problems.

For my *second* suggestion, I would like to consider the national attitudes that bear on the great problem of peace. I hope you will not think me amiss if I turn to my own country and certain rather special circumstances found there to illustrate my point. Despite the amazing conquest of the air and its reduction of distances to a matter of hours and not days, or minutes instead of hours, the United States is remote in a general sense from the present turbulent areas of the world. I believe the measure of detachment, limited though it is, has been of help in enabling us on occasion to take an impartial stand on heated international problems.

Also, my country is very specially constituted in terms of population. We have many families of Norwegian ancestry in our population. My country also includes large numbers of former citizens of many of the other countries of Europe, including the present satellite states. I recall that when the first Polar flight was made by the Russians from Moscow over the top of the world to land on the little airfield of the post I commanded at Vancouver on the Columbia River in the state of Washington, my home was surrounded within a few hours by hundreds and hundreds of Russians, all presumably citizens of the United States. Italians, Turks, Greeks, and many, many others who came to our country now constitute an organic portion of our population.

From this fact we have acquired, I think, a feeling and a concern for the problems of other peoples. There is a deep urge to help the oppressed and to give aid to those upon whom great and sudden hardship has fallen.

We, naturally, cannot see a problem in the exact terms as people like yourselves or the Danes, or the Dutch, or the French, for example—people living in the closest contact with each other, yet widely differing in national heritage. I believe there is, however, a readiness to cooperate which is one of the great and hopeful factors of the world of today. While we are not in close contact with the details of problems, neither are we indifferent to them, and we are not involved in your historical tensions and suspicions.

If I am correct in thinking that these factors have given us as a nation some advantage in the quest for peace, then I would suggest that principles of cooperation based on these factors might contribute to a better understanding amongst all nations.

I realize fully that there is another side to this picture. In America we have not suffered the destruction of our homes, our towns, and our cities. We have not been enslaved for long periods, at the complete mercy of a conqueror. We have enjoyed freedom in its fullest sense. In fact, we have come to think in terms of freedom and the dignity of the individual more or less as a matter of course, and our apparent unconcern until times of acute crisis presents a difficult problem to

the citizens of the countries of Western Europe, who have seldom been free from foreign threat to their freedom, their dignity, and their security. I think nevertheless that the people of the United States have fully demonstrated their willingness to fight and die in the terrible struggle for the freedom we all prize, to sacrifice their own men in large numbers for this common cause, and to contribute vast sums for the general benefit of the Western countries.

I recognize that there are bound to be misunderstandings under the conditions of wide separation between your countries and mine. But I believe the attitude of cooperation has been thoroughly proven. I also believe that the participation of millions of our young men and women in the struggle in Western Europe, in the closest contact with your people, will bring as its result less of misunderstanding on our side of the Atlantic than perhaps on yours.

In my own case, for example, I spent two and one half years in France during the First World War. Frequently I was quartered in the households of the French peasantry and spent long evenings by the kitchen fires, talking far into the night. I came to know them well, admired them, and in some cases came to love them. Now, how many do you suppose of the present citizens of Western Europe have had a similar look-in on the homes of people in the farms and small towns of America. A few may know much

of New York, Washington, and Chicago, but those great cities do not represent the heart of America.

The *third* area I would like to discuss has to do with the problem of the millions who live under subnormal conditions and who have now come to a realization that they may aspire to a fair share of the God-given rights of human beings. Their aspirations present a challenge to the more favored nations to lend assistance in bettering the lot of the poorer. This is a special problem in the present crisis, but it is of basic importance to any successful effort toward an enduring peace. The question is not merely one of self-interest arising from the fact that these people present a situation which is a seed bed for either one or the other of two greatly differing ways of life. Ours is democracy, according to our interpretation of the meaning of that word. If we act with wisdom and magnanimity, we can guide these yearnings of the poor to a richer and better life through democracy.

We must present democracy as a force holding within itself the seeds of unlimited progress by the human race. By our actions we should make it clear that such a democracy is a means to a better way of life, together with a better understanding among nations. Tyranny inevitably must retire before the tremendous moral strength of the gospel of freedom and self-respect for the individual, but we have to recognize that these democratic principles do not flour-

ish on empty stomachs, and that people turn to false promises of dictators because they are hopeless and anything promises something better than the miserable existence that they endure. However, material assistance alone is not sufficient. The most important thing for the world today in my opinion is a spiritual regeneration which would reestablish a feeling of good faith among men generally. Discouraged people are in sore need of the inspiration of great principles. Such leadership can be the rallying point against intolerance, against distrust, against that fatal insecurity that leads to war. It is to be hoped that the democratic nations can provide the necessary leadership.

The points I have just discussed are, of course, no more than a very few suggestions in behalf of the cause of peace. I realize that they hold nothing of glittering or early promise, but there can be no substitute for effort in many fields. There must be effort of the spirit—to be magnanimous, to act in friendship, to strive to help rather than to hinder. There must be effort of analysis to seek out the causes of war and the factors which favor peace, and to study their application to the difficult problems which will beset our international intercourse. There must be material effort—to initiate and sustain those great undertakings, whether military or economic, on which world equilibrium will depend.

If we proceed in this manner, there should develop a dynamic philosophy which knows no restric-

tions of time or space. In America we have a creed which comes to us from the deep roots of the past. It springs from the convictions of the men and women of many lands who founded the nation and made it great. We share that creed with many of the nations of the Old World and the New with whom we are joined in the cause of peace. We are young in world history, but these ideals of ours we can offer to the world with the certainty that they have the power to inspire and to impel action.

I am not implying in any way that we would attempt to persuade other people to adopt our particular form of government. I refer here specifically to those fundamental values on which our government, like many other democracies, is based. These, I believe, are timeless and have a validity for all mankind. These, I believe, will kindle the imagination and arouse the spirit.

A great proponent of much of what I have just been saying is Dr. Albert Schweitzer, the world humanitarian, who today receives the Nobel Peace Award for 1952. I feel it is a vast compliment to be associated with him in these awards this year. His life has been utterly different from mine, and we should all be happy that his example among the poor and benighted of the earth should have been recognized by the Peace Award of the Nobel Committee.

I must not further complicate this discussion with the wide variety of specific considerations which

will enfold the gradual growth of a sound approach toward some method of securing an enduring peace in the world. I fear, in fact I am rather certain, that due to my inability to express myself with the power and penetration of the great Churchill, I have not made clear the points that assume such prominence and importance in my mind. However, I have done my best, and I hope I have sown some seeds which may bring forth good fruit.

OF STATECRAFT AND WAR

Bruce Jones and Will Moreland

The first and great purpose of statecraft is to avoid wars that are unnecessary, ill-considered, or unjust. This is also an essential purpose of an effective defense; no less a leader than George Washington argued: "To be prepared for war is one of the most effective means of preserving peace." But this does not mean that all wars can be avoided. We live in a world where statesmen and stateswomen must navigate amid conflicting national interests as well as the actions of opportunists and populists, adventurers, and the genuinely evil. The moral statesperson will exhaust the options of diplomacy and statecraft first, but must be prepared to go to war and to risk the many consequences of conflict when confronted with genuine threat or evil.

The men and women who crafted and implemented the Marshall Plan in the wake of World War II, and who built the United Nations (UN) and the North Atlantic Treaty Organization (NATO), needed no such reminders. They had gone to war to fight against both direct threats and evil, and 60 million people perished in the process. In the aftermath of the war, which itself followed a failed effort to rebuild from the great slaughter of World War I, these leaders turned to statecraft to prevent a similar fate from befalling a future generation.

The world they confronted was unlike ours in almost every way. Europe was ravaged by six years of fighting, devastated both physically and economically. Asia was exhausted by the fight against Japanese conquest and adventurism, and China was mired in a brutal civil war. The United States had come through the Second World War with a newly dominant position in the world, and it is important to remember today that the war was won with the essential help of Stalin's Russia. The challenge was to rebuild after a cataclysmic struggle.

Few of the economic or political features of that moment resemble the world of today. The world's population in 1945 was 2.36 billion; today it stands at 7.35 billion.[1] The total global economy was by 1950 (after some recovery) $9.99 trillion (in 2016 U.S. dollars); today it stands at $73.43 trillion, and the degree of economic and social connections between coun-

tries far outstrips that in the interwar period or in the aftermath of WWII.[2] And that is to say nothing of more recent trends we now take for granted, including globalization, rapid cultural changes, or the worldwide adoption of digital technology.

And yet, as different as our world is from that which General George Marshall and his colleagues surveyed, there are surprising echoes of their moment in what confronts us today. There are similar themes, most of all, in the challenges that statecraft must steer us through if we are to avoid the risk of a new crisis resulting in a violent disordering of the world around us. Then as now, American diplomats, working with friendly nations, had to craft a vision of order and an architecture to support it: a set of relations among states and peoples and the instruments and institutions of collective security, of common defense, and of cooperation between states. To be sure, we have many such arrangements now, several of them designed by Marshall and his postwar colleagues—but even a casual survey reveals that they are ill-adapted to today's threats.[3]

The conservative impulse to learn from history does not always guide us well, but a careful reading of history can illuminate lessons and judgments that can inform effective statecraft. That was true for that postwar moment, seventy years ago, when our predecessors adapted the tools of statecraft to the business of rebuilding a shattered world while successfully

avoiding another great war. Of course, today's powers are not those of the 1940s. There are limits to history's lessons. But the Marshall Plan era does remind us that we have struggled before to define a system—an architecture of principles, rules, and institutions—through which to try to collaborate with powers whose political systems are not our own and who distrust our intentions, just as we, increasingly, distrust theirs.

The lessons of the Marshall Plan era are three. First, they are about the importance of tying American power to the defense of democracy. This is a lesson often neglected today, notably in endless debates about whether our European allies spend enough on their own defense. Second, the lessons are about the need to act economically and not just militarily to shore up friendly states. This lesson is echoed in contemporary negotiations over the Trans-Pacific Partnership but too often forgotten with the obsessive focus of recent debates about American leadership on military intervention in the Middle East and naval power in Asia. And third, the lessons are about the merits of forging lasting institutions and arrangements for security and tending to those arrangements—rather than leaving our security to ad hoc, usually temporary, approaches. By applying these principles, George Marshall, Dean Acheson, and others of their era crafted a set of arrangements that kept America and Europe safe during the long

cold war with the Soviets, kept the peace in Asia, and laid the foundation for dynamic economic growth, both in the Western world and in East Asia.

A WORLD AT RISK

What world do we currently confront, and what are the demands of statecraft today? For five decades after the Second World War, global politics was structured around the confrontation between the United States and the Soviet Union—around the effort to avoid having the cold war turn hot. After the collapse of the Soviet Union, two things happened. First, the open economic arrangements shaped by the United States and adopted in Europe in the wake of World War II (what we call the liberal economic order) spread far beyond its Western core, bringing into a shared global economy countries as diverse as China, Brazil, India, and Vietnam—as well as Russia. Today's globalization is a function of that integration.

Second, in the absence of a direct threat from the Soviet Union, the two peace and security institutions established by Marshall and his colleagues evolved well beyond their initial purposes. Put simply, the UN went in and NATO went out. In the post–cold war era, the UN increasingly deployed inside countries' borders to help quell civil wars in places ranging from Cambodia to Mozambique. NATO, no longer absorbed with the Soviet threat, confronted a need to go "out of area

or out of business." The alliance soon deployed, well beyond its basic writ of territorial defense, to the Balkans and then out of the European theater entirely to help tackle wars in West Asia. The UN and NATO efforts achieved decidedly mixed results.

These were the institutional manifestations of a deeper phenomenon: the articulation and then the collapse of the American unipolar moment.[4] That moment was both exceedingly brief and exceedingly ill-managed. From 1990 to 2008 the United States had no peer competitor and faced no existential threat, although of course it was attacked at home by al Qaeda in 2001. By 2008, despite the advantageous U.S. position, American military power was bogged down in both Iraq and Afghanistan, and Wall Street and government regulators had together failed to anticipate or prevent a global financial crisis that originated in the United States. These were not decisive blows to American power, but they did dent the perception of American dominance. After the financial crisis in particular, Washington was compelled to turn to the emerging markets—those countries that had profited most from the post–cold war spread of the U.S.-backed economic order—to help shape and finance the rescue of the global economy.[5]

These events gave new support for the notion of American decline and contributed to the emergence of a multipolar order comprising both the West and the BRICS (Brazil, Russia, India, China, and South

Africa). At the core of the notion of a multipolar world were two competing ideas. One was convergence: that the emerging powers were likely to see it in their own best interests to adopt the core provisions of the liberal international order forged under President Harry Truman, and as a result they would contribute responsibly to global affairs. Some argued that China, in particular, would grow into being a "responsible stakeholder."[6] The alternate view was of a drift into a "G-Zero world" of "everyone for themselves" in which no actor would dominate.[7] U.S. strategy over the past decade has been premised on the first assumption and oriented toward avoiding the second.

Reality has looked different. The argument about the emerging powers failed to see critical differences between them. Brazil is not China and India is not Russia. In the period after 2009, these differences became both more pronounced and more consequential. The reemergence of an adventurous authoritarianism in Russia, manifested in the 2014 seizure and annexation of Crimea, is the most obvious and flagrant aspect of this. Over time, the emergence of a more assertive Chinese stance under President Xi Jinping may prove the more consequential. Meanwhile Brazil has lapsed into internal political confusion (probably only temporarily), and India, still growing, has begun to lean in an American direction—but how enduringly is open to debate.

Thus in 2017, seven decades after the crafting of the Marshall Plan, we see the following features of the international system. The United States is still the only truly global power, but it is mired in political and conceptual uncertainty about its role.[8] Russia is acting to reassert its role as a global power with the military but without the economic capabilities to support that stance. China continues to expand economically but at a slower rate than in the previous two-plus decades and is increasingly assertive in international security terms, both in its region and beyond. The bloc of emerging powers continues to exist both diplomatically and on development issues, but it remains a non-force on economic and strategic questions. And the Middle East has entered into what is sure to be an extended stretch of crisis and of war. A long period of democratic and economic consolidation in Latin America and Africa is ebbing, though not yet in reversal.

In this moment, there are surprising echoes of the half-decade between 1944 and 1949 when the United States faced a choice as to which pathway it would follow. It was a period in which, then as now, the question was whether liberal powers and illiberal powers could collaborate on the administration of economic recovery and cooperate on the management of international security. In that 1940s moment, a cold war became the answer.

MARSHALL, TRUMAN, AND THE CHALLENGE
OF GREAT POWER COOPERATION

When Marshall, Truman, and their colleagues strategized about American power, they faced challenges parallel to our own. The Europe of today is, of course, much richer and more stable than the Europe of the 1940s; there is no comparison. But the events of 2009 to 2016 have shown that despite the concentration of economic wealth and democratic political institutions in Europe, democracy is more fragile than imagined just a few years ago. Extreme right-wing sentiment is reemerging in Europe at an alarming pace and with surprising vigor, destabilizing core precepts of the pan-European project. Soft authoritarians in the vein of Hungary's Viktor Orban openly aspire to creating "illiberal new state[s] based on national foundations," raising doubts as to Europe's democratic future.[9] Such instability creates space for political, economic, and—on Europe's border—even quasi-military penetration by Russia. Marshall would have recognized the challenge of consolidating democracy in Europe, and he would have appreciated the challenge of helping an Eastern Europe threatened by a Russian power seeking to impose its vision of economic and political order on what it considers its sphere of influence.

More broadly, Marshall would also have recognized the choice we face on whether or not to seek

to cooperate with authoritarian or semi-authoritarian powers. Today that choice presents itself in terms of confronting the illiberal powers when they seek to impose influence through pressure and force, while cooperating with them when we can tackle common enemies like radical Islamic terrorism.

Strobe Talbott's foreword to this book recalls the basic story of the events that drove the need for the initiation and the conceptualization of the Marshall Plan, as well as Brookings's roles in crafting that initiative. To see more fully the parallels to the contemporary challenge, we need to bring forward an additional strand, to highlight what came before the Marshall Plan—that is, an alternative vision for the reconstruction of Europe through the establishment of the UN Relief and Rehabilitation Agency (UNRRA), as part of a larger vision of the UN structure for management of the postwar world.

From 1941 onward, American and British diplomats and policy planners began to turn their attention to winning the peace. As early as 1942, Brookings's Leo Pasvolsky was brought into the War and Peace Studies Group, a confidential unit within the State Department dedicated to postwar planning.[10] Over the course of the subsequent year, Pasvolsky and his team wrote the first draft of what would become the United Nations Charter. Even before the Bretton Woods and Dumbarton Oaks conferences that gave birth to the World Bank and the Treaty of San Fran-

cisco, which created the United Nations, Pasvolsky's colleagues, led by Assistant Secretary of State Dean Acheson, developed the basic structure of the United Nations Relief and Rehabilitation Administration, which was to begin preparing for the reconstruction of Europe and other war-savaged theaters.

Underlying this activity was President Franklin Delano Roosevelt's vision of a world made secure by the "four policemen." An evolution of his original "Big Three" concept, this was a great-power pact between the United States, the United Kingdom, Nationalist China, and the Soviet Union, the four pillars of the Allied coalition of World War II. It was a vision of spheres of influence with the United Kingdom guaranteeing the security of Western Europe and its own still-global empire, the Soviet Union securing Eastern Europe and Central Asia, China maintaining order in East Asia, and the United States securing the Western Hemisphere. To this quartet, Winston Churchill later insisted on adding France; that quintet survives to this day as the five permanent members of the UN Security Council (minus, for the most part, the spheres of influence).

In the European context this compact among the powers was due to take the form of the UNRRA serving as the leading entity for the reconstruction of Europe, with the Americans and the Soviets cooperating on that effort. But by the time the war had ended in the summer of 1945, Roosevelt had died and

the concept of the four policemen was much less certain. Harry Truman replaced Roosevelt, and a vision of the world governed by great-power cooperation had begun to falter, as Soviet-American relations deteriorated, with the two sides advancing opposing visions for postwar Europe.

For four fateful years, summer 1945 to summer 1949, these two visions of the world played out in parallel. In one world, the architecture for security was grounded in the United Nations and its Security Council, embodying the great-power concept. In this world, the United States and the Soviet Union would continue as allies and work together through the UNRRA to ensure the reconstruction of Europe.

Yet through 1944, the ambassador to Moscow, Averell Harriman, detected a clear hardening of Soviet attitudes, reflecting Moscow's ideas for the postwar future. Following Roosevelt's death in April 1945, he flew to Washington specifically to brief President Truman on what he perceived to be an increasingly hostile and intransigent Soviet Union. The ambassador put it in stark terms, describing the United States as facing a "barbarian invasion of Europe."[11] Over the course of the coming two years, Truman would sour on Roosevelt's vision and eventually, after many twists and turns, adopt a more hardline position about Soviet spheres of influence than that which Roosevelt had agreed with Stalin at the Yalta Conference.

For the remainder of this four-year period, the UN architecture would be put in place even as the core relationship meant to hold it together would unravel. In late 1945 the UNRRA became an official agency of the newly formed UN organization born out of the San Francisco treaty. The UN's sister institutions, the International Monetary Fund and World Bank, were created in December 1945. While these developments appeared to show concrete progress in Soviet-American cooperation, U.S. skepticism was on the rise. In September 1945 the defection of Igor Gouzenko in Ottawa revealed not only a sizable Soviet spying operation in the United States and Canada but the fact that the spy ring was after the United States' most guarded secret—the details of its atomic arsenal.[12] Doubts about Soviet intentions and sincerity grew.

On February 9, 1946, Joseph Stalin gave a speech in which he asserted that capitalism made future war inevitable, drawing sharp distinctions between the Soviet and the Western worldviews. Peaceful coexistence, to say nothing of collaboration, seemed off the table.[13] Confronted by urgent calls from Washington for an explanation, George Kennan, then U.S. chargé d'affaires in Moscow, penned his influential "Long Telegram" analyzing Stalin's stance in the context of Russian imperial history and arguing for "resistance" to Soviet aggression. The negative momentum gathered.

As 1945 flowed into 1946, skepticism around Soviet intentions had grown among Soviet watchers monitoring the Soviet presence in Iran. Moscow and London had jointly occupied the country in 1941, but the Soviets were consistently delaying their withdrawal, despite private discussions between Stalin and Secretary of State James Byrnes, as well as American pressure in the Security Council. By the end of 1945, it seemed apparent to U.S. Soviet expert Charles Bohlen that Moscow "did not intend to honor this treaty."[14] This suspicion was confirmed in March 1946 when the United Kingdom withdrew its forces from Iran and the Soviets let that deadline slide by as well.[15] Churchill, watching this, alongside additional Soviet movements across Eastern Europe, famously proclaimed "an iron curtain" descending over eastern Europe.

At first, though, Churchill's speech was received with widespread critique and doubt. The United States continued to invest in the UN. Even when confronted with Soviet espionage targeting the American nuclear program, the Truman administration sent special envoy Bernard Baruch to present a plan for joint UN control of nuclear weapons at the first session of what was then called the UN Atomic Energy Commission (which would later become the International Atomic Energy Agency).[16] The Soviets finally withdrew their forces from Iran under intense diplomatic pressure—including President Truman's

redeployment of the U.S. Sixth Fleet to the eastern Mediterranean.[17] Truman was still exploring Roosevelt's vision for an inclusive architecture, while at the same time considering a narrower alliance.

MARSHALL AND THE PIVOT TO NATO

In January 1947 George Marshall, well known to the American public as the "architect of victory" for his role as wartime Army chief of staff, assumed the position of secretary of state. Marshall had already proved his diplomatic chops in a two-year mission to China as Truman's special envoy. Upon moving into the new State Department building in Washington's Foggy Bottom, Marshall embarked on a series of negotiations with the Soviets about the European question, especially around German reconstruction. Six weeks of intensive negotiations between Marshall and Soviet foreign minister Vyacheslav Molotov failed to bridge their differences.

Much of their debate was over the principles that would govern the reconstruction of Germany and wider Europe. The first stages of this task had been undertaken by the UNRRA. Beginning in 1943 with the liberated countries of the Balkans and expanding to cover all of Europe by 1945, the UNRRA brought together forty-four countries to coordinate immediate relief support for Europe's civilian population.[18] Evolving out of an initial promise by Chur-

chill to assist a liberated France, President Roosevelt later pressed for an internationally coordinated effort to plan, coordinate, administer, or arrange for the administration of measures for the relief of victims of war in any area under the control of any of the United Nations. This was to be done by providing food, fuel, clothing, shelter, medicine, and other basic necessities.

Here too, Roosevelt sought to employ his four policemen model. The organization that emerged in November 1943 revolved around a central committee composed of the United States, the Soviet Union, the United Kingdom, and China.[19] The UNRRA was in essence the test-case for the four policemen concept, two years before negotiations over the UN Charter. Some even heralded the organization of the "first blueprint of the post-war order."[20]

The composition of that initial blueprint was fiercely debated. Though Roosevelt eventually settled on shaping the directorate around the Big Four, Washington at first proposed a wider and more inclusive format. Resistance quickly emerged from the other three powers—the Soviets and Chinese wanting to retain as much centralized control as possible, and the British concerned that too large a body would suffer the same sclerosis that had beset the League of Nations.[21] The Americans were quick to acquiesce to the demands of the other three; Assistant Secretary of State Acheson, then leading the delegation,

actively supported the UNRRA as a vehicle for great-power cooperation, to the point of endorsing UNRRA aid to the Soviet Union.[22] This ambition that the UNRRA would be a unifying factor was widely echoed; contemporary scholar Philipp Weintraub praised the value of the institution as "a nonpolitical international body whose activities are not to be used as a political weapon."[23]

Events, however, would rapidly unfold in a different direction. In May 1947 it was the United States, not the UNRRA, that provided $400 million to Greece and Turkey to aid their rebuilding. It was also the United States that provided guarantees to Greece about its security in the face of broiling civil war.[24] Soon after, in a June 5 speech at Harvard University, Marshall laid out a broad outline for an American-led, not UN, option for Europe—the European Recovery Program (what would become colloquially known as the "Marshall Plan").[25]

Growing strategic concerns and mistrust underlay this shift. Washington increasingly viewed the Soviets as violating the neutrality that undergirded the UNRRA by politicizing aid to achieve Moscow's security aims. (Of course, America's strategy also had a political aim: using aid to resist communism.) By December 1946 Acheson had lost faith in the prospects for the UNRRA and reversed his public support, going so far as to announce U.S. opposition to further UNRRA aid to countries that were rearming

or using food as political weapons. UNRRA director Fiorello La Guardia (more famous for his previous tenure as mayor of New York) singled out the following offenders: Byelorussia, Ukraine, Yugoslavia, Czechoslovakia, Poland, and Albania.[26]

The March–April 1947 Council of Foreign Ministers Conference in Moscow laid the final groundwork for the American shift to what would become the Marshall Plan. Secretary Marshall traveled to Moscow hoping to make concrete progress on issues of German economic reconstruction and peace treaties with Berlin and Vienna. For five weeks, Marshall wrangled with the British, French, and Soviet delegations, meeting particular obstinacy from Molotov on every issue. Finally electing to speak directly with Stalin, Marshall found the Soviet leader seemingly equally apathetic about progress.[27] To Bohlen, at Marshall's side as adviser and translator, the secretary concluded Soviet lethargy was deliberate policy:

> [Stalin's] attitude impressed General Marshall very much indeed. He talked about it all the way back to the Embassy and all the way back to Washington on the plane. General Marshall felt that Stalin was obviously waiting for Europe, harassed and torn by the war and in virtual ruins, to collapse and fall into the Communist orbit.[28]

The State Department's strategic planners appreciated the dangers here. Economic deprivation was the root threat in Europe; as George Kennan would later note in a 1947 policy planning paper, Europe's woes stemmed from "profound exhaustion of physical plant and spiritual vigor."[29] Containing communism would require containing the pains from hunger and cold of winter. The United States could not remain trapped in endless Soviet games; it would have to step forward on its own.

Yet even then, with this change in view under way throughout 1946–47, the idea of cooperation with the Soviets was not completely abandoned. Through June and July 1947, intensive negotiations in Europe progressed over the implementation of the nascent Marshall Plan, including delegates from Eastern Europe. Many in the State Department doubted that these nations would successfully join the European Recovery Program; they faced the double challenge of a Moscow that could not condone U.S. influence in the Soviet sphere of influence and a U.S. Congress that would balk at the idea of funding communist governments. Nonetheless, the potential participation of the Soviet-occupied countries still spoke to the American strategy of pursuing a universal architecture, or, at least, being seen to pursue a universal architecture so that the resulting architecture would be as wide as possible. Driven by a humanitarian impulse, if there was even a chance that a divided nation

like Czechoslovakia could participate, it was worth extending the hand.

Furthermore, even the *realpolitik* rationale that the United States did not want to be viewed as responsible for erecting barriers and sinking the universalist vision reveals the idealism upon which the American-led architecture was being built. Washington did not want to alienate countries by being held responsible for dividing the world. As Bohlen recalls Marshall fretting at the time: "If we don't include [the Eastern European states], it obviously looks like an anti-Soviet measure and we'll lose a lot of support throughout the world."[30] The fact that the United States wanted the support of those countries demonstrates the critical distinction between the emergent Eastern and Western blocs: where the former would be based on coercion, the latter would be founded on the consent of those participating nations.

Consequently, as the negotiations unfolded in Paris, U.S. representatives were eager to engage the Eastern Europeans—though this came at considerable political expense on the home front. The American Congress was wary. With the war's end, the American public grew increasingly reluctant to provide financial assistance to partners and allies. The wartime lend-lease to the Soviets came to an abrupt conclusion in May 1945. Even Britain, arguably the closest wartime ally, found U.S. support for additional financial assistance was limited; confronted with the need

for a $6 billion loan at the end of its own lend-lease program, London was met with tough demands from U.S. negotiators to end the system of British imperial preferences. What was even less anticipated though, both in Whitehall and Foggy Bottom, was the subsequent strident opposition to the eventual $3.75 billion loan package from Congress and the public.[31]

Only months before Marshall's Harvard address, President Truman, in a March speech unveiling his eponymous doctrine, had called for the United States to help "free and independent nations to maintain their freedom."[32] Debate immediately followed as many in the fiscally conservative Congress recoiled at the potential of overseas aid expenditures at a time when the U.S. government was making deep cuts in its domestic budget. Even as, in the words of Dean Acheson, the administration sought to galvanize support by making the threat of communism "clearer than the truth," senators continued to resist, on one side questioning the expense of foreign commitments and, on the other, recoiling at the chance that any funding would go to communist-controlled countries and thereby aid "the enemy." Public opinion was also a constraint; after the huge sacrifices of the Second World War the American public was in a mood to concentrate on "nation-building at home"—a concern with strong echoes in our era.

Ultimately, after several weeks of domestic hand-holding, Moscow's leaders solved Marshall's congres-

sional problem for him when they made clear to the East European states that participation in the Marshall Plan would incur retribution from the Soviet Union.[33] The door to an open architecture was slammed shut, but Washington had successfully made sure it was not the one to close it. Growing antagonism from the Soviets helped the Truman administration with public opinion too, as officials increasingly used anticommunist rhetoric to make the case for sustained engagement in Europe.

For Moscow, a sphere of influence in Eastern Europe was more important than economic reconstruction, especially when the focus of Soviet leaders was on extracting significant reparations to rebuild their own economy rather than revitalizing Europe. As a result of the gulf between the Soviet and American concepts, relations rapidly eroded. The Soviets sought to offset the U.S. narrative that Moscow had been the one to divide Europe, taking to the pulpit at the UN to decry the Truman Doctrine and the Marshall Plan as antithetical to the UN system.[34] By early 1948 Western opinions on the Soviet menace hardened with the communist coup in Czechoslovakia in February, followed by the suspicious death of Foreign Minister Jan Masaryk in March.[35] By the end of that month, the United Kingdom, France, Belgium, Luxembourg, and the Netherlands would join together in a mutual defense treaty that formed the Western Union Defense Organization, a security mecha-

nism designed to bolster their conventional defense against a Soviet military strike.[36] Only days later, Soviet representatives walked out of the Allied Control Council, the forum designed to coordinate the management of postwar Germany. The last vestiges of cooperation between the wartime allies continued to fray as the continent divided. Finally, and fatefully, in June the Soviets embarked on their last-ditch effort to hamper Anglo-American plans to begin rebuilding the western portions of Germany by announcing a blockade of Berlin. In response, America began its famous Berlin airlift.

Shaken by the Soviet use of military power to thwart the West's economic agenda, Marshall began to move forward on a transatlantic security architecture. Instructing Robert Lovett, his old wartime deputy and new undersecretary of state, to begin secret talks with European and Canadian ambassadors on a set of collective defense arrangements, Marshall accepted an argument long brewing within a portion of the State Department—that conventional security and economic security could not be divorced.[37] Europe's economic recovery depended not only on financial assistance but also on a sense of physical security that underlies confidence in one's government and society. A stable and free Europe, for which America had just fought in order to maintain its own security, would require that U.S. leaders avert the mistakes of the last war and make a commitment to preclude an-

other conflagration. Though it would be under the leadership of Dean Acheson, Marshall's former right hand and successor, this project was brought to fruition in April 1949 with the creation of the North Atlantic Treaty Organization. At its core, however, it was Marshall's prescience in connecting security and economics—over the vehement disagreement of several Soviet experts in the State Department—that laid the foundation for the U.S. cold war strategy and, arguably, the eventual European project.[38]

Yet, even as they were building a transatlantic security architecture, which would serve as the cornerstone of the cold war "West," Marshall and his colleagues did not entirely turn their backs on the United Nations. Indeed, the UN would not wither altogether; it is with us to this day. And in what may be a foreshadowing of today's realities, while the UNRRA and Soviet-American cooperation had broken down in Europe, the UN remained relevant in other regions and formats. In the Middle East, the outbreak of war between Israel and the Arab states in 1948 thrust the United Nations into political negotiations and peacekeeping operations, with U.S. and Soviet cooperation.[39] This is forgotten by today's policy planners and foreign policy thinkers, but the UN then evolved to be the primary tool of crisis and conflict management in the Middle East, through the early 1970s. Furthermore, though Europe's postwar economic reconstruction was driven by the Mar-

shall Plan not the UNRRA, that did not stop both Moscow and Washington from agreeing in 1949 to the formation of the Expanded Program of Technical Assistance—the precursor to the UN Development Program—for economic development in the former European colonies that were just beginning to achieve independence. Over the course of the next two decades, UN development agencies would help usher into statehood much of the postcolonial world, reshaping the global political landscape—and along with it, the politics of the UN itself, which was eventually sidelined by the clash between the West and the new developing world.[40]

DO MARSHALL'S LESSONS APPLY TODAY?

Fast forward to the present day. Though the landscape is different, we see an essential parallel on questions related to whether the liberal powers (at least the United States, Europe, Canada, and the Asian democracies) can choose to structure international architecture in a way that allows and encourages the Chinese and Russians to cooperate—or whether the Chinese and the Russians will choose to pursue their own paths. Is a modern-day version of the four policemen model possible? Or will great-power cooperation once again founder on self-interest and the desire for spheres of influence?

Is there an alternate vision of great-power coop-

eration that does not sacrifice the political independence of smaller states? Or will we once again see a pattern of confrontation in Europe and perhaps in Asia? And will that coexist with partial cooperation in the Middle East?

We can hear the echoes of Pasvolsky, Marshall, and Acheson in today's debate over whether we can resist the Russians in their moves to dominate Ukraine while cooperating with them in the shared fight against Islamic terrorism. The fights over economic reconstruction in Eastern Europe and what it would mean for the balance of power between the Soviets and the West resonates in today's debate over the European Union's role in Ukrainian political and economic reform. Similarly, a reminder of the U.S. postwar concerns arises in our considerations of whether we can cooperate with the Chinese economically while resisting their efforts to create a sphere of influence in East Asia.

We see the commonalities between the architecture of the Marshall Plan and that of the Trans-Pacific Partnership—both American-led economic blocs, but open to participation by non-allies, including, potentially, China in the case of the TPP. Just as the aid provided by the European Recovery Program was defined in part by European requests, not just American fiat, so the terms of TPP have resulted from negotiations among (relatively) equal stakeholders. But just as the Soviets withdrew cooperation from

the Marshall Plan, seeing it as limiting their search for a sphere of influence, so the TPP is increasingly viewed both in China and the United States as a strategic effort to use economic power to constrain—not contain—the Chinese.

In fact, we should hear these echoes of Marshall and Pasvolsky more clearly than we do. The parallels between the world they confronted and the one we now face have been muted in current debates about American leadership. These debates have been narrow in scope, often confined to the question of U.S. military intervention, especially in the Middle East. This is an important question, but it is not the core question of statecraft or the architecture needed to keep the peace. The U.S. foreign policy discussion has been dominated and distorted by debates around the decision to go to war in Iraq and its implementation. The shadow of that war has remained, permeating the discussion around the Obama administration's more intensive focus on diplomacy and the president's avoidance of the use of force in the case of Syria.

While the United States has been deliberating its military strategy in the Middle East over the course of two presidencies, China was rising and pulling the Russian economy up with it through its demand for raw materials. And while Putin's Russia is a shadow of its 1944 self, China stands apart as a far more substantial actor than it was at the end of the Second World War—or arguably at any time since the

eighteenth century. So, we still confront two non-Western powers with potentially divergent visions for international order, though with a reverse in the geography: The Asian power is strong and growing stronger still; the European power is weak, though capable of tremendous damage. Each in a very different way still seeks something resembling a "sphere of influence"—an area where each can dominate political developments—and that remains fundamentally at odds with the U.S. outlook.

When this challenge arose in 1944–49, the wisdom of the U.S. approach was its flexibility in leading the creation of a dual-track architecture where it could engage at differing depths to maintain stability between the great powers without sacrificing progress on American security and values. The question now is whether a similar approach to today's challenges is feasible.

Of course, the Russia and China of today differ from each other as much as they differ from Stalin's Soviet Union and Nationalist China; they have distinct strategies for dealing with the international system. Of China it is sometimes said that it is, or can be, a constructive power globally but a revisionist power regionally. China's September 2015 commitment to the UN of 8,000 peacekeepers and $1 billion stands in contrast to its island building in the South China Sea.[41] Chinese economic ambitions in Europe and on-off cooperation with the United States on North Korea somewhat

complicate that narrative. The bigger point is this: to draw a narrow authoritarian/democratic divide between the West and China is simplistic and misleading.

China is confronting its own internal struggles on the authoritarian/democratic divide and thus is walking both sides of that aisle. To date it has managed to defy gravity, simultaneously deepening its economic openness while tightening its grip on domestic political dissent and the media. Although this "foot-in-two-camps" strategy appears unsustainable, others have predicted a breakdown before and repeatedly been proven wrong. It is still true that China is deeply integrated into the global economy. Through the 2000s, it was assumed that this fact would help to manage strategic competition, and while strategic competition is mounting it is still the case that the economic codependency between the United States and China puts ballast in the relationship that helps slow growth of those tensions.

Russia, by contrast, is a genuinely authoritarian power, and one that has been defying gravity in a very different way: continuing to invest in a massive military re-armament and engaging in adventurism in its surrounding region, even as its economy suffers under low oil prices and U.S.-EU sanctions.[42] Russian president Vladimir Putin is quick to rattle his saber when confronted by opponents and has demonstrated little regard for civilian casualties in his military escapades. He presides over a regime that, much

like his Stalinist predecessors, grows more and more dependent on the perception of external threats to retain public support.

Thinking about the lessons of the UNRRA/ Marshall Plan debate, and bringing those lessons forward to the present day, it seems likely that America's strategy on Russia and on China should each reflect a version of this dual track approach, but in obverse ways. When it comes to China, it is hard to see any real alternative but to adopt Marshall's and Pasvolsky's experiment of parallel strategies: one for Chinese inclusion and another for cohesion among allies—but in China's case, we should lean forward on the prospects for inclusion. Today's parallel is the simultaneous negotiation of the Bilateral Investment Treaty that would deepen cooperation between the United States and China, while following through on the Trans-Pacific Partnership—an arrangement theoretically open to China but more realistically a tool for constraint.[43] As we pursue this course, though, it is important to remember the core lessons of the Marshall era: that U.S. power is bound to the democratic character of the states that it seeks to protect, and the political and democratic character of our friends and allies must be shored up economically as much as, or perhaps more than, militarily.

With Russia, the obverse strategy seems more credible. By the time Russia sent military forces to Syria, in defiance of UN and U.S. efforts to nego-

tiate a common political pathway forward (however wan that effort was), it was clear that Russia had decided to close the door on cooperation with the West. There have been intense debates since about whether the expansions of NATO and the EU, along with the placement of the American missile shield in Europe (which, in actuality, does nothing to interfere with the flight path of Russian missiles to the United States), had so threatened Russia that it had no choice but to turn away from integration with the West.[44] These claims are unconvincing, but even if accurate they do not change the fact that the West held open the door to cooperation with Russia through the entire course of the post–cold war period. History will tell that it was Russia that closed the door. The Russians have not slammed it shut though; a crack remains. And so the obvious strategy in the case of Russia is to shore up allied defenses and deterrence, but to build a pathway back to cooperation should Russia choose to pursue that approach at some point.

Across both cases, we should remember the argument that U.S. strategy is wisely tied to institutions of architecture, of burden sharing and cooperation both with the West and beyond. The contemporary fashion for ad hoc coalitions leaves much to be desired in how these mobilize the political and planning support of our allies. Particularly, such temporary coalitions provide no mechanism for institutional memory, losing lessons acquired over years of cooperation and

offering no means to build trust among parties. Additionally, they fail to signal a lasting American commitment to a region or problem.

And because great-power tensions can spill over into crisis in the Middle East, we need tools to lower tension. We do not yet know whether the American, Russian, and Chinese strategies in the Middle East will follow the 1947 pattern, or whether a different game will unfold. Between 1947 and 1973 we saw a consistent pattern as various states in the Middle East confronted one another militarily, each of them U.S. or Soviet clients. Crises unfolded, risking escalation between the Soviet Union and the United States. When things risked getting out of hand, as they often did, the United States and the Soviet Union came together at the United Nations to negotiate ceasefires, impose them on their clients, and deploy UN peacekeepers to stabilize lines of separation and cessation of hostilities.

We see an echo of this pattern in the contemporary Middle East and could see more. That kind of great-power cooperation has already been important for nonproliferation, notably in the P5+1 (the permanent five members of the Security Council and Germany) negotiations over Iran. We might see deeper echoes of the earlier pattern if the United States chose to wield its power in a more assertive way in Syria. In the post-Obama era, we might see a synthesis between the George W. Bush administration's too-frequent

failure to craft an overarching diplomatic strategy for its use of force and the Obama administration's too-frequent failure to recall that the credible threat of the use of force can be a tool of effective diplomatic strategy. As Kennan once succinctly put it: "You have no idea how much it contributes to the general politeness and pleasantness of diplomacy when you have a little quiet armed force in the background."[45]

If the 45th president does pursue such a path, we may see a situation where the United States offers a more effective diplomatic strategy for Syria; and we may end up with Russian, American, and other forces deployed in Syria to try to stabilize that brutal civil war under the joint umbrella of the United Nations. This is not conflict resolution and peacebuilding of the kind that has come to characterize UN interventions in civil war. It is merely conflict suppression— but through the 1950s, 1960s, and 1970s, suppressing local and regional conflicts in the Middle East repeatedly helped avert a global war.

HISTORY'S RHYMES

At Brookings today, no longer at its wartime Lafayette Square address but now anchoring think tank row on Massachusetts Avenue, we often think on the period between 1944 and 1949 when a UN world was dreamed up and attempted, and a NATO world was born in the wake of the UN's early failures.

Many contemporary Brookings scholars grew up during the cold war when NATO underlay Western security. Some began their careers in the post–cold war era—that moment during which the fall of the Soviet Union left the United States unfettered on the world stage and Washington, at least for the first part of that period, chose to wield its power in large part through multilateral institutions, especially the UN. Some of us saw first-hand the extraordinary results that can occur when the great powers choose to use force through international institutions. Those working in an international organization can never be blind to the reality that such institutions are instruments of the great powers, not agents of order in their own right (though the academic literature often misses this point). But when those powers choose to wield them, they can be important instruments of a more humane world.

It is unlikely that we still live in such a world. The U.S.-Russian clashes over Ukraine and Syria and the return to proxy war are likely harbingers of much that is to come. But at least for the moment, like Pasvolsky, we will argue for pursuing dual paths in parallel, testing and refining the proposition that there may be some issues on which liberal and illiberal powers can cooperate, while not giving ground on the central principles for which our predecessors fought. That will require much more nuanced strat-

egy than we've recently witnessed vis-à-vis China, and much more resolve in dealing with Russia.

As the rhetoric of the American presidential campaign of 2016 made clear, we also may soon confront a world in which the United States itself chooses not to act effectively on the world stage. In a return to its inward-looking posture of the pre–World War II era, the United States could choose to walk away from the principles and practices that have kept it safe ever since that war. If the United States does make a fateful choice to abandon the alliances it helped create and to try to build walls against the international economy, those who make that choice and those who support it will carry the blame, first and foremost, for what we believe will be violent disordering that will almost certainly follow.[46]

At least a portion of that blame, though, will fall on those who have forgotten that the essential purpose of statecraft is to avoid war, not to promote it. As it will to those who have complained to our European allies about their failure to spend enough on their own defense, while at the same time failing to explain clearly to the American public about the stake we have in the democratic character of Europe. As it will to those who neglected the lessons that the political character of our allies and friends matters, instead tying us to thugs and dictators and making it harder to convince the American public of the purpose of

the alliance structure. As it will to economic planners who forgot in the pursuit of growth that economic strategy should first and foremost reinforce democracy—in this country above all. And as it will to those who forgot that American power inherently inspires both awe and fear, making the binding of U.S. power to a rules-based architecture a crucial reassurance to a world that can be frightened by American power. In short, a share of responsibility will fall on those of us who focus on the strategic and tactical aspects of foreign policy and international economics, while failing to prevent the erosion of understanding in the United States about the merits of the current international system or the need to adapt it more profoundly to contemporary circumstances.

NOTES

1. Esteban Ortiz-Ospina and Max Roser, "World Population Growth," Our World in Data 2016 (https://ourworldindata.org/world-population-growth/).

2. GDP 1950 figures are from Angus Maddison, "The World Economy, 1950–2001," in *The World Economy: Volume 1: A Millennial Perspective* and *Volume 2: Historical Statistics*, OECD Publishing, 2006 (http://dx.doi.org/10.1787/9789264022621-20-en). Current world GDP comes from the World Bank at http://data.worldbank.org/indicator/NY.GDP.MKTP.CD.

3. In a forthcoming volume in Brookings's The Marshall Papers series, Jones looks more carefully at what instruments of security architecture we need now to confront the world in which we live. In parallel Jones and Moreland hope that others will turn their attention to the question of how the global eco-

nomic system can be made more inclusive and thus more politically sustainable. As we do so, the wisdoms and the failings of
George Marshall, Leo Pasvolsky, and their colleagues should be
very much on our minds.

4. For further reading on the "unipolar moment," see its origins in Charles Krauthammer, "The Unipolar Moment," *Foreign
Affairs* 70, no. 1 (1990/1991). Further assessments can be found
in William Wohlforth, "Unipolarity, Status Competition, and
Great Power War," *World Politics* 61, no. 1 (January 2009), 28–57;
and Robert Jervis "Unipolarity: A Structural Perspective," *World
Politics* 61, no. 1 (January 2009), 188–213.

5. For an overview of the international response to the 2008
financial crisis and the greater inclusion of the emerging markets through the G-20, see Daniel Drezner. *The System Worked*
(Oxford University Press, 2014).

6. This phrase was first popularized by Deputy Secretary
of State Robert Zoellick in a 2005 speech: Robert Zoellick.
"Whither China: From Membership to Responsibility?" Delivered to National Committee on U.S.-China Relations in New
York City. September 21, 2005 (http://2001-2009.state.gov/s/d/
former/zoellick/rem/53682.htm).

7. The G-Zero scenario was first outlined by David Gordon
and Ian Bremmer in 2008. Bremmer's 2012 book, *Every Nation for
Itself: Winners and Losers in a G-Zero World* (New York: Portfolio,
May 2012), elaborates on this subject.

8. For an analysis of the United States' lasting status as the
leading global superpower, see Jones's 2014 book, *Still Ours to
Lead: America, Rising Powers, and the Tension between Rivalry and
Restraint* (Brookings Institution Press, 2014).

9. Colin Woodard, "Letter from Budapest: Europe's New
Dictator," *Politico*, June 17, 2015 (www.politico.com/magazine/
story/2015/06/hello-dictator-hungary-orban-viktor-119125).

10. Robert Schulzinger. *The Wise Men of Foreign Affairs: The
History of the Council on Foreign Relations* (Columbia University
Press, 1984), 60–61.

11. John Lewis Gaddis, *George F. Kennan: An American Life*
(New York: Penguin Press, 2011), 192.

12. For an account of Gouzenko's defection and the subsequent trials and public reaction, see Amy Knight, *How the Cold*

War Began: The Igor Gouzenko Affair and the Hunt for Soviet Spies (New York: Carroll and Graf Publishers, 2005).

13. "Vladislav Zubok on Stalin's 1946 Speech," *American Experience*, PBS (www.pbs.org/wgbh/amex/bomb/filmmore/reference/interview/zubok3.html).

14. Charles E. Bohlen, *The Transformation of American Foreign Policy* (New York: W.W. Norton & Company, 1969), 78.

15. Martin Walker, *The Cold War: A History* (New York: Henry Holt and Company, 1993), 41.

16. Randy Rydell. "Going for Baruch: The Nuclear Plan That Refused to Go Away," Arms Control Association (www.armscontrol.org/act/2006_06/LookingbackBaruch).

17. John Lewis Gaddis, *The Cold War: A New History* (New York: Penguin Press, 2005), 28.

18. Keith Lowe, *Savage Continent: Europe in the Aftermath of World War II* (New York: Picador, 2013), 106.

19. Agreement for United Nations Relief and Rehabilitation Administration (57 Stat. 1164; Executive Agreement Series 352).

20. Grace Fox. "The Origins of the UNRRA," *Political Science Quarterly* 65, no. 4 (December 1950), 561 (www.jstor.org/stable/2145664?seq=1#page_scan_tab_contents).

21. Ibid., 577.

22. Robert Beisner. *Dean Acheson: A Life in the Cold War* (Oxford University Press, 2009), 29.

23. Philipp Weintraub, "UNRRA: AN Experiment in Social Welfare Planning," *Journal of Politics* 7, no. 1 (February 1950), 9.

24. David McCullough. *Truman* (Simon and Schuster, 1993), 553–54.

25. The text of Marshall's speech (also published in this volume), along with considerable analysis on the address and public response, can be found via the George C. Marshall Foundation at http://marshallfoundation.org/marshall/the-marshall-plan/marshall-plan-speech/.

26. Beisner, *Dean Acheson*, 46.

27. For a full account of Marshall's time at the Moscow Council of Foreign Ministers meeting, see chapter 12 in Forrest C. Pogue, *George C. Marshall: Statesman 1945–1959* (New York: Viking, 1987), 168–96.

28. Bohlen, *The Transformation of American Foreign Policy*, 88.

29. Tony Judt, *Postwar: A History of Europe Since 1945* (New York: Penguin Press, 2005), 89.

30. Bohlen, *The Transformation of American Foreign Policy*, 91.

31. David McLellan, *Dean Acheson: The State Department Years* (New York: Dodd, Mead & Company, 1976), 70–73.

32. "The Truman Doctrine," Address before a Joint Session of Congress by President Harry S. Truman, March 12, 1945 (http://avalon.law.yale.edu/20th_century/trudoc.asp).

33. Ed Cray, *General of the Army: George C. Marshall, Soldier and Statesman* (New York: W. W. Norton and Company, 1990), 615.

34. Jussi Hanhimäki and Odd Arne Westad, eds., "Vyshinsky Speech to the United Nations General Assembly, September 1947," in *The Cold War: A History in Documents and Eyewitness Accounts* (Oxford University Press, 2004).

35. Gaddis, *The Cold War*, 32–33.

36. Gaddis, *George F. Kennan*, 304.

37. Cray, *General of the Army*, 663–64.

38. George Kennan, for one, vehemently opposed the formation of NATO. See Gaddis, *George F. Kennan*, 325–34.

39. Bruce Jones, "The Security Council in the Arab-Israeli Conflict," in *The Security Council in the 1990s*, David Malone, ed. (Boulder, Colo.: Lynne Reinner, 2004).

40. For an account of the progression of the Expanded Program of Technical Assistant to UNDP, see UNDP's history at "On Its 50th Anniversary, UNDP Is Looking towards the Future, 2016" (http://50.undp.org/en/#timeline).

41. For an overview of China's actions in the South China Sea, see the Council on Foreign Relation's "China's Maritime Disputes" (www.cfr.org/asia-and-pacific/chinas-maritime-disputes/p31 345#!/p31345). At the United Nations in September 2015, President Xi Jinping announced an expanded peacekeeping commitment; details can be found at Nikhil Sonnad. "China Climbs the UN Peacekeeper Charts by Committing 8,000 Troops," *Quartz*, September 29, 2015 (http://qz.com/512865/china-climbs-the-un-peacekeeper-charts-by-committing-8000-troops/).

42. After the beginning of the Ukraine crisis in 2014, Moscow continued to increase its defense spending until March 2016, when falling oil costs forced a 5 percent decrease in a 3.14 trillion-ruble defense budget. See Paul Sonne, "Low Oil Prices Force Russian Defense Cuts, Top Military Business Boss Says," *Wall Street Journal*. March 10, 2016 (www.wsj.com/articles/low-oil-prices-force-russian-defense-cuts-top-military-business-boss-says-1457656937).

43. Under negotiation for eight years, the U.S.-China Bilateral Investment Treaty would remove barriers to investment and market access between the United States and China. For American firms, such an agreement would open sizable sections of the Chinese economy that Beijing has kept blocked off from foreign investment. For greater details, see Shannon Tiezzi, "Are China and the US Close to Sealing an Investment Treaty?," *The Diplomat*, March 24, 2016 (http://thediplomat.com/2016/03/are-china-and-the-us-close-to-sealing-an-investment-treaty/).

44. For an entry point into this debate, see the article and response in John Mearsheimer, "Why the Ukraine Crisis Is the West's Fault," *Foreign Affairs* 93, no. 5 (September/October 2014), and Michael McFaul, Stephen Sestanovich, and John J. Mearsheimer, "Faulty Powers: Who Started the Ukraine Crisis." *Foreign Affairs* 93, no. 6 (November/December 2014).

45. Gaddis, *George F. Kennan*, 241.

46. For a detailed accounting of the dynamic that may follow American retrenchment, see Robert Kagan, *The World America Made* (Knopf, 2012), or Thomas Wright, *All Measures Short of War: The Contest for the 21st Century and the Future of American Power* (Yale University Press, 2017).

THE
GREEN MAN

Spirit of Nature

JOHN MATTHEWS

CONNECTIONS
BOOK PUBLISHING

For Ari Berk, wizard of the green pen

A CONNECTIONS EDITION
This edition published in Great Britain in 2002 by
Connections Book Publishing Limited
St Chad's House, 148 King's Cross Road
London WC1X 9DH
www.connections-publishing.com

British Library Cataloguing-in-Publication Data available upon request.

ISBN 978-1-85906-067-4

9 10

Phototypeset in Goudy Old Style BT using QuarkXPress on Apple Macintosh
Printed in China

Contents

PART ONE

The
Coming of the
Green Man

LEFT *The face of the Green Man gazes down from a medieval roof boss in Norwich Cathedral, Norfolk, England.*

You may not know it, but you have almost certainly seen more than one Green Man in your lifetime. If you have visited any of the magnificent Gothic churches scattered over much of Europe, even as a curious tourist, you will have seen the wonderful carvings known as foliate heads – faces which seem human but which, when examined closely, appear to be made of leaves. Or, you may have wandered into a museum and seen some of the fine medieval tapestries which depict scenes from the lives of some strange-looking, leafy figures known as Wildmen. These, too, are green men – as is the figure of Robin Hood, the famous outlaw of Nottingham's Sherwood Forest, or the wonderful figure of Puck in Shakespeare's *A Midsummer Night's Dream*. Here, as elsewhere, the Green Man lurks, almost in hiding, staring out from amid the trees of the Forest of Arden, or laughing down from the high transepts of cathedral roofs.

'all who come in contact ... feel changed by the encounter'

But just who is this being, and what relevance can he possibly have for us today? The answer to this question leads us into some odd places, many of them well off the beaten track, for the story of the Green Man is made up of many strands, each of which contributes to the whole. For some the

6

Green Man is an ancient symbol of nature and fertility, who can be seen to represent humankind's connection with the earth. To others he is a symbol of wildness, of the untamed spirit which lives within us all and reflects the wildness at the heart of nature. In our own time the Green Man has become an unofficial icon for the environmental movement, pointing to the way in which we continue to interact with the world around us. One thing is certain: all who come in contact with this extraordinary and powerful being feel changed by the encounter.

SPIRITS OF THE TREES

The idea of the Green Man as a representative of the natural world probably dates back to the first agrarian peoples of ancient times, who felt the power of nature and gave it a face and form. We have only to look at the way in which greenness thrusts through, rampantly overcomes, and glories in its strength to understand why a masculine image was chosen. Certainly, among the tribal people who lived in the vast woodlands that once covered much of the European continent the Green Man

A Wodwose, or Wildman, from a medieval tapestry in St Anna Kloster, Bruch, Germany.

ruled supreme as a spirit of these woods, a representation, in semi-human guise, of the abiding life-force of the trees.

Both as an actual presence and as symbolic entities in their own right, the vast woodlands made a deep and lasting impression on the imagination of those who dwelt close to their shaded depths. Individual sacred trees featured in many cultures and often possessed the qualities of the deities to which they were dedicated. Though no truly ancient image of this kind has survived, we may imagine that certain trees could have been seen as representatives of the Green Man, and may well have been carved into his likeness. Even if this were not the case, the connection between trees and the sustaining of the world provided links with the energy of nature which the Green Man embodied.

For the Norse people, the entire world was founded on the roots and branches of the World Tree, Ygdrasil, while in ancient Ireland, the great yew, Eo Mugna, was considered a source of Druidic and territorial power. In the Mediterranean world, the cult of the dying-and-rising god Attis – himself a type of Green Man – was represented by a pine tree, which was borne in procession.

> '*a representation, in semi-human guise, of the abiding life-force of the trees*'

In a severely deforested world, it is hard to imagine just how dense our woodlands once were. Forests were places of awe and mystery, into whose depths few would dare to venture during the day, although the resources of the woodshore were useful to all those who lived nearby. In North-west Europe, these dense forests often contained groves of sacrifice or spiritual mystery; both human and animal offerings were hung from trees in the groves dedicated to the Norse cult of Odin, indicators of the

This woodland sculpture from Stewart Park in Middlesbrough, England, shows the Green Man as the guardian spirit of the trees.

powerful force of the ancient forest gods. The oak groves of the Celtic world were the haunt of strange forest beings and awesome tree-spirits, their mysteries known only to the Druids, whose knowledge and understanding of the natural world was second to none.

THE WILDMAN IN THE GREEN

Wildness, and a passionate energy, are an essential part of the Green Man's character. Leaf-mask carvings discovered in the Middle Eastern cradle of civilization lead us to the Sumerian epic of Gilgamesh (c. 700 BCE), in which we encounter a figure who represents just such a power: Enkidu, a wild and primitive being whose great strength and passionate soul embodies the energy of nature itself.

Jealous of his power, the gods condemn Enkidu to die, prompting his friend, the hero Gilgamesh, to undertake a journey to the otherworld in search of a cure for death itself, in the form of a plant called 'The Old Man has Become a Young Man Again'. Although Gilgamesh finds the plant, he then loses it once more to a serpent, which immediately sloughs its skin in a symbolic image of rebirth.

'the haunt of strange forest beings and awesome tree-spirits'

11

In the poems which make up the Gilgamesh epic, Enkidu symbolizes an overflowing life-force, wild and untamed. He stands out as one of the oldest representations of the potent energy of the Green Man which was later to reappear – during the Middle Ages – in the figure of the Wildman, who represented a return to the idea of living closer to the natural world.

'a return to the idea of living closer to the natural world'

GREEN OSIRIS

In ancient Egypt, where water was scarce and the annual rising of the Nile waters was essential to all life, green gods and goddesses played an important part in the spirituality of this ancient land. The colour green was honoured above all, and to 'do green things' came to mean doing good, while to 'do red things' meant to do evil. Osiris, perhaps the most important deity in Egyptian life, was both a god of vegetation and resurrection. In the Pyramid Texts, he is known as 'The Great Green' and is depicted as green-skinned in acknowledgement of his life-giving energy.

The story of Osiris told of his murder and dismemberment at the hands of the jealous god Seth. Afterwards, his wife (and sister) Isis recovered the scattered parts of his body and restored him to life. Thereafter, this cycle of dismemberment, death and resurrection was honoured as a symbolic reference to the flooding of the Nile delta, by which the fields were greened with new growth when the waters rose. In token of this, miniature mummy cases representing Osiris were sown with grain and left out in the rain until they sprouted – an emblematic statement of life rising from death, and a perfect expression of the energy that flowed in the veins of the Green Man.

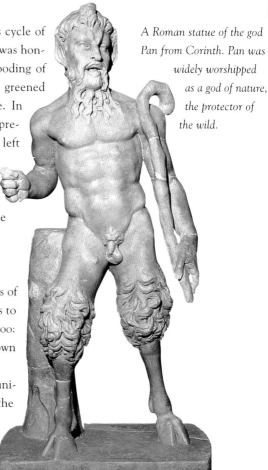

A Roman statue of the god Pan from Corinth. Pan was widely worshipped as a god of nature, the protector of the wild.

PAN AND GREEN DIONYSUS

In the classical world, the orderly deities of Mount Olympus were not the only ones to hold sway. There were older, wilder forces too: every tree, stream, hill and grove had its own dryad, nymph and tutelary spirit.

The god Pan, whose name means 'universal', was a major deity of nature. As the protector of the wild, he could appear anywhere in the natural world. Those

13

The laughing face of the Green Man keeps watch from the external timbers of Samlesbury Hall, North-west England.

who came across him at lonely, unfrequented places were said to be consumed with panic at the sight of him. This experience of solitude, of a numinous sense of wild, god-filled nature, is one seldom experienced in a world that has tamed so much of the earth. But Pan could not be tamed or controlled, any more than Dionysus (Roman Bacchus), another representative of unfettered nature, could be made to obey the desires of his followers.

Before his later association with vines and drunkenness, Dionysus is credited with the fostering of agriculture among the Greeks, and his power often manifests in images of growth and wildness. At one point he is said to have undertaken a journey to India, spreading the word about the intoxicating power of the vine. During the journey he was captured by some sailors, who tried to ransom him for a vast sum, but Dionysus caused a huge vine to grow out of the deck of their ship, and ivy and vines to twine throughout the rigging. The oars became serpents and the whole ship was filled with animals, with Dionysus, in lion form, as their leader.

The wild green power of Dionysus, like that of Pan, overcomes the ordered world of humanity in much the same way that plants penetrate concrete. His growths overwhelms man-made structures, and his ferment enters into the human body so that we can experience for ourselves the ecstatic life of plants. Both gods represent an energy which forms an essential aspect of the Green Man.

THE GREEN ONE

In Arabic culture, green is the colour of rebirth and resurrection, and is the spiritual colour of Islam. Paradise is said to be green, and the twelfth, or 'hidden', imam – a spiritual leader who will one day emerge to benefit the world – is described as living on a Green Island. There are also references in the Koran to 'Al-Khidir', or 'The Green One', a figure whose origins can be traced back to an ancient vegetation cult but who was later described as a spiritual guide to both Moses and Alexander the Great. He lives outside time and is therefore immortal, having dived into the Well of Life.

In the Arab world, green thus represents divine wisdom, and those who either bear its colour or are symbolically associated with it are especially holy. To this day, Muslims who make the pilgrimage to the source of their spirituality in the holy city of Mecca wear green in token of their devotion.

'his power often manifests in images of growth and wildness'

15

*The god Krishna dances
with musicians in this
seventeenth-century
tapestry from Rajasthan.*

THE GREEN MAN IN THE EAST

Throughout the Far East, deities of blue or green skin abound, these colours being perceived as representing life. In India, the blue-skinned Krishna is hailed as the preserver of life and bears the title 'The Supreme Pervader'. Associated with the first months of spring, he destroys pain and brings ecstatic communion with the heavenly realms. Like the Greek Orpheus or the Southwest American Kokopelli, Krishna brings delight to the earth through music.

An early avatar of the god Vishnu, Rama, is often shown with dark-green skin. Rama lives within the woods and takes as his wife Sita, who springs up from the ground when the earth is ploughed. Sita is a goddess of nature, and when Rama becomes her consort the two reign over the natural world together. Such is Rama's beauty that the Hindu scriptures say birds, beasts, animals, insects and trees long to draw near him, and fall ill when they are unable to do so.

'a need for images of greenness ... the lineage of the primal Green Man'

Such images and stories tell us that the Green Man, under whatever guise or title, flourished throughout the East every bit as much as in Europe. In each case there was a need for images of greenness and, when these images became identified with specific deities, they were – in their own way – continuing the lineage of the primal Green Man.

OPPOSITE *This classical Green Man, with leaves for hair, is found on a fountain in Piazza Pietro d'Illi Ria, Rome.*

THE SPROUTING MASKS

Some of the oldest concrete images of the Green Man date from the second century CE, in an area once part of the vast Mesopotamian Empire but by then ruled over by the Romans. These early images are little more than male masks with leaves sprouting from them, which appear on fountains and at the bases of temple columns, but they may have been influential in the appearance of one of the most clearly developed expressions of the Green Man to be found anywhere in the world.

These are the astonishing, rich and varied faces, seemingly made of leaves or peering out from a screen of vegetation, which flourished among the carvings that decorate both the inside and outside of medieval churches and cathedrals from the twelfth century onwards. There, the face of the Green Man – half human, half vegetation, sometimes laughing, sometimes fierce, almost always slightly mocking – grins down from on high. Carved on hundreds of roof bosses, finials and the bases of columns, he is a pagan image peering out from the stone forests of Christianity.

'half human, half vegetation, sometimes laughing, sometimes fierce'

18

FORESTS OF STONE

During the Middle Ages, woodlands were managed and coppiced to provide cover for deer and sport for the nobility. Forests were administered by royally appointed foresters and wardens, and became forbidden to ordinary people. But the loss of the forests and the building of the great cathedrals coincide.

'lore and imagery became embodied in dance, story, song and legend'

The Church tried to teach people that the woods were full of evil from the start, but it was partly in acknowledgement of the importance of the ancient treescapes that so much of the architecture of medieval churches was designed to make them look like stone forests. It is not surprising to find the Green Man there; his presence was too deeply embedded in the consciousness of the ordinary people to be forgotten.

But other factors underlie the Green Man carvings of the Middle Ages. The dependency upon the harvest had not yet been replaced by modern methods of preservation and freezing. If the harvest failed, so did life – no one was exempt. The construction of the great cathedrals entailed the cutting down of prime trees to provide scaffolding for the huge stones to be raised. This enormous undertaking required its own harvest of men, skilled craftsmen who learned their trade through respect for their materials – stone, iron and wood. It was they who carved the foliate heads and placed them high above the heads of the worshippers. And, like all men engaged in dangerous work, they needed their talismans, carving their protectors in places of honour in acknowledgement of their powers. For the first time men had climbed higher than ever before. Were they aware of the hubris of climbing higher than the tallest trees, even in the service of God's glory? Lest the woodland spirits be offended, their green images were set higher than the holy images upon the altar.

This foliate head from a fourteenth-century font in Tostock Church, Suffolk, England, hides its face among the leaves.

Ideas and realizations of this kind passed into the folk-life and customs of ordinary people, along with the distant memories of devotion to the power of nature. Scraps of lore and imagery became embodied in dance, story, song and legend, underpinning the traditions of a world that still acknowledged the presence of the Green Man despite an increasing sense of separation from nature.

PART TWO

Myths and Traditions

LEFT *Men in leafy costumes entertain the court in this fifteenth-century illustration from* Chronicles of France *by Froissart.*

The Green Man has continued to reappear throughout the ages, reflecting – in the way he is represented and in the forms he takes – the changing relationship of humanity with nature. Often, and not suprisingly considering our constant attempts to subdue the earth to our needs, he comes as a challenger, seeming at times more than a little threatening. Yet beneath this fearsome aspect lies an unquenchable fountain of delight, which finds outlet in many ways – notably the exuberant festivals of May Day and Midsummer, which continue to be celebrated to this day, and which periodically become an all-out honouring of the Green Man in his many forms.

THE GREEN YEAR

Like many of the gods of the ancient world, the Green Man is ever-present in the cycle of the growing year. He makes his youthful appearance amid the first green unfurling of spring, growing sturdily into the full panoply of summer manhood before beginning his descent into the rich reds and browning tints of his autumn age. As the bare, withered branches of winter reveal the skeletal woods, he remains present in the evergreens of the forest. The Green Man is a constant companion throughout the year, and his presence is acknowledged at the many festivals which celebrate the turning of the seasons.

'beneath this fearsome aspect lies an unquenchable fountain of delight'

As the emerging green of early spring covers winter's bareness, it is time to herald the beginning of summer with festivals which celebrate Maytime. The Green Man appears now as the King of the May, whose consort is chosen from the fairest maidens of the village. At this time the Green Man is young and desirous – the bringer of fertility and ecstatic celebration. When summer's basket is replete, he reappears as the mature Harvest King, his beard full-grown, echoing the full ears of standing grain in every field. Then he is cut down with ritual solemnity, his sacrifice becoming the stored bounty of barns, the flour to make bread, the grain to ferment beer and distil spirits.

When the cold blasts of winter blow the last leaves from the trees, his spirit returns as the King of the Winter Woods. His celebrations are fearsome games and contests, full of riddles, wrestling and combat. At the hub of the winter-locked wheel of the year, his games provide the vigour to spin the wheel of life once more – to begin the cycle of green growth without which we could not live. His pastimes literally pass the dead time of midwinter, making us grateful for his gifts which keep us alive when all else is dead.

Giuseppe Arcimboldo's riotous sixteenth-century painting of a man made from fruits and greenery, commissioned by Emperor Maximilian II, embodies the essence of the Green Man.

25

OPPOSITE *The Green Man spits forth leaves in this carving from a fourteenth-century roof boss in St Andrew's Church, South Tawton, Devon, England.*

KINGS OF THE WOOD

From earliest times the ancient pattern of planting, growth and harvest was supported by rituals designed to ensure that the yearly cycle continued. At one time sacrificial offerings – often human – were made to appease the gods of the natural world and ensure the health and fertility of the earth. In many parts of the world, especially throughout the Mediterranean, vegetation and harvest cults sprang up with their attendant mysteries of the dying-and-rising god. One of the most widespread stories focused on the sacrificed god-king, sometimes called the 'King of the Wood' or 'Rex Nemorensis' – a man chosen to reign for a year, then killed, his slayer taking over his role for a further twelve months.

A variation on this theme incorporated a ritualized battle between the king and his successor – now identified as the Kings of Summer and Winter – for the possession of the Maiden of Spring (more about this on the following pages). These three characters and their story reappear in literature and folklore all over the world, and in each case if we look closely we can see the face of the Green Man peering out from behind these characters of myth and legend.

'if we look closely we can see the face of the Green Man peering out'

26

Robin Hood and his Merry Men entertain Richard the Lionheart in Sherwood Forest, in this nineteenth-century painting by Daniel Maclise.

ROBIN HOOD

A figure who unites the characteristics of the sacrificial Year King with the spirit of the forest and woodland is Robin Hood. Better known as the leader of a band of twelfth-century outlaws in Sherwood Forest, he is in fact a far more complex, myth-based character, whose historical existence is at best doubtful, but whose life, as told in medieval ballads, follows a universal pattern.

Of unknown or doubtful parentage, Robin appears fully fledged, living in the greenwood with his outlaw band, the Merry Men. Their trickster-like adventures, which conceal a darker historical truth in which Norman overlords ruthlessly oppressed their Saxon serfs, marked them out as semi-divine beings hiding behind the appearance of medieval freedom fighters.

The eventual death of Robin Hood, betrayed and bled almost to death by a priestess-like figure, shows him to be a type of Rex Nemorensis, while Marian, Robin's greenwood sweetheart, represents the Queen of the May, a figure as old as the Green Man himself, decked out in flowers and garbed in white. Together, these two ancient beings ruled over the riotous May Day games – often referred to as Robin Hood's Games – which celebrated the arrival of spring with a wildness and abandon that is very much an embodiment of the Green Man.

The appearance, from the height of the Middle Ages, of Robin, Marian and the Merry Men in the folk-plays of Britain makes it clear that their true nature was recognized by the ordinary people, who continued to celebrate the mysteries of the green year in this way under the suspicious eyes of the Church.

'Their trickster-like adventures ... marked them out as semi-divine beings'

ROBIN GOODFELLOW AND PUCK

Robin Hood's trickster-like activities link him with another dweller of the greenwood – Robin Goodfellow, who not only shares his name and nature with the famous outlaw, but draws him firmly into the circle of fairy lore.

Robin Goodfellow is perhaps better known to us as Puck, the wild and uncontrollable spirit of Shakespeare's *A Midsummer Night's Dream*, but behind this disguise lurk far older figures, dating back beyond the Middle Ages. Famous for their jokes and jests – mostly at the expense of foolish humans – these are the primordial trickster gods who appear in mythology all

'forest spirits whose

volatile presence

can still be felt in

the deep woodlands'

over the world. The function of these beings was to challenge human self-limitation and to lead us to grow and develop. They taught by paradox and trickery, forcing us to take paths into unknown territory.

Both Robin Goodfellow and Puck survive in the shape of, among others, the Bucca in Britain and the Bosgou of North-west Spain. These are forest spirits whose volatile presence can still be felt in the deep woodlands, but who never bid harm either to creatures of the wild or humans humble enough to acknowledge their own animal natures. This, too, is a function of the Green

Man, whose presence constantly reminds us of our relationship to the green world, and challenges us to maintain it in the face of a perpetual trend towards subduing nature to our own needs and desires.

THE GREEN KNIGHT

The challenge offered to us by the Green Man is wonderfully portrayed in a great fourteenth-century poem, *Sir Gawain and the Green Knight*. In this we meet another of the Green Man's many avatars, and learn something of the strengths and weaknesses contained within humanity.

The story, which is set in the Arthurian world, opens as King Arthur and his court are sitting down to dinner. A loud crash of thunder and a flash of lightning announce the coming of a strange and terrifying figure; the description declares him to be a Green Man (see overleaf):

The Green Knight raises his severed head before King Arthur and the court, in this illustration from the fourteenth-century poem Sir Gawain and the Green Knight.

From his neck to his loins so square set was he, and so long and
stalwart of limb, that I trow he was half a giant. And yet he was a
man, and the merriest that might ride. His body in back and breast
was strong, his belly and waist were very small, and all his features
    full clean.
Great wonder of the knight
Folk had in hall, I ween,
Full fierce he was to sight,
And all over bright green.

This powerful and threatening figure offers to play a 'Christmas
game' in which he will exchange blows with any man there, on condition that whoever gives the blow will accept a blow in return.
Gawain alone has the courage to face the giant, and with the Green
Knight's own axe cuts off his head. To the horror of all the company,
however, the monstrous visitor rises and, taking up his head, holds
it aloft. The lips move and the voice speaks, telling Gawain that he
must journey to the Green Chapel one year hence to receive back
the blow he has given.

As the seasons turn, Gawain sets out in search of the Green
Chapel and is given shelter at the castle of Sir Bercilak, who tells
Gawain that the place he is seeking lies close at hand, and offers
him hospitality and a guide when the day of the trial dawns. During

OPPOSITE *The Green*
Man turns his eyes toward
heaven, in this carving
from St Michael's Church,
Warfield, Berkshire,
England.

this time, Gawain is unknowingly tested by Lady Bercilak, who attempts to seduce him three times. On the last attempt Gawain accepts a talisman from her which she claims will protect him from the Green Knight's axe.

On the appointed day Bercilak provides the promised guide to the Green Chapel. The Green Knight appears, and Gawain kneels to receive the blow. Twice his adversary feints, then mocks Gawain's courage. Finally, he nicks Gawain's neck and declares himself satisfied. To Gawain's astonishment, the Knight then reveals he is really Sir Bercilak, and that he and his wife were placed under enchantment by 'the Goddess Morgane', whom Gawain had seen disguised as an ugly old woman in the castle. The whole episode had been set up to test the courage of Arthur's court, and Gawain in particular. The only reason for the slight wound to Gawain's neck was because he had failed at the last and accepted the protective talisman.

The Green Knight's game is an age-old one. The god offers his life-blood for the sake of the people, in return for their own courage and self-sacrifice. This exchange is at the heart of the Green Man's story. As the guardian of the natural world he challenges people to acknowledge his yearly sacrifice by offering a willing service to all of creation. Gawain does not overcome the Green Knight but submits to a strength greener than his own.

THE BATTLE OF WINTER AND SUMMER

Underlying both the Robin Hood myth and the story of the Green Knight is a far older myth – that of the battle between the Kings of Summer and Winter for possession of the Spring Maiden. This theme goes all the way back to the rituals of the Year Kings and the Rex Nemorensis, and underpins a vast cycle of myth and legend from many different cultures. The two combatants, or their champions, fight annually for the hand of the Maiden, and also for rule over the opposing halves of the year. As the pattern of the seasons always follows the same path through the yearly cycle, there can only ever be one outcome – the King of Summer must defeat the King of Winter

and win the heart of the Maiden of Spring. But, since the natural progression of the seasons was not always perceived as inevitable, the ritual enactment of the struggle of one against the other was regarded as a serious event, and this is reflected in the myths which describe it.

Foliate heads sprout from a tree held aloft in this sixteenth-century bench-end carving from St Mary the Virgin, Bishops Lydeard, England.

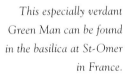

Thus in the cycle of Robin Hood myths, the battle is replayed in Robin's continuing struggle with his arch enemy, the Sheriff of Nottingham, while in the Gawain poem the hero's contest with the Green Knight harks back to the older battle, with – in this instance – Lady Bercilak carrying the role of the Spring Maiden, and Gawain acting as the champion of the Summer King (Arthur) against Bercilak as the Winter King.

JACK-IN-THE-GREEN

The presence of figures like Robin Hood and Maid Marian in the European folkplays and the festivals of May Day and Midsummer bears witness to the continuing presence of the Green Man. Another such figure is the Green Jack, or Jack-in-the-Green, a wild and sometimes comical figure who accompanies the dancers and minstrels at many of these seasonal celebrations. In most instances he is represented by a man carrying a framework made from woven

This especially verdant Green Man can be found in the basilica at St-Omer in France.

branches and leaves, sometimes bedecked with flowers. This often heavy costume covers both head and body, so that it gives the appearance of a moving bush or tree.

Often the Green Jack is led about through towns and villages by groups of supporters, who collect money to pay for the celebrations in this fashion. One account, which describes the celebration of Garland Day in the town of Castleton in Derbyshire, England, shows that a darker theme underlies the procession. Here, the Garland King is led through the streets on horseback. On reaching the local church the framework of greenery and flowers is hooked up to a winch, which then hauls it to the top of the tower, where it is left to swing in the wind until the elements gradually demolish it. At one time, it was most likely a sacrificial victim whose body or head – was carried aloft, perhaps to swing from the topmost

'Jack-in-the-Green, a wild and sometimes comical figure'

A mischievous leafy head adorns a bench end in Winchester Cathedral, Hampshire, England.

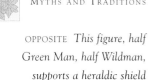

OPPOSITE *This figure, half
Green Man, half Wildman,
supports a heraldic shield
in the William Tell chapel,
Vierwaldsee, Switzerland.*

branches of a tree. Such things link more recent folk-traditions with a far older time, when the propitiation of the gods of nature was a much more serious business.

Although we may see such celebrations in a different light today, they still, nevertheless, describe the spirit of the forest emerging from the wildwood and coming into the streets and among the houses to be hailed and honoured. When men cover themselves with leaves and align themselves with the green spirit of growth, this sacred showing has its own element of uneasiness. Such over-lapping margins, where civilization and wildness meet, are tinged with awe and an uneasy hilarity that tries to cover the fear that can be woken by such epiphanies of greenness in anthropomorphic form.

WILDMEN IN THE GREEN

Another aspect of the spirit of nature and the wild-wood, whose function is not unlike that of the Green Jack, is the Wildman. Descriptions of him abound in medieval literature, where he is usually seen as a man who combines human, animal and, sometimes, vegetative traits. Usually covered with long hair or leaves, and always fierce and

*'combines human,
animal and, sometimes,
vegetative traits'*

A Wodwose climbs above an arch in the porch of Peasenhall Church, Suffolk, England.

'the Wildman remains a part of the celebrations of the folk-year'

ungovernable, these strange beings are often shown carrying a club, or even an uprooted tree, with which they will thrash about at the slightest sign of human approach.

The medieval writers who described these creatures saw them as representatives of nature untamed – beings who had rejected human civilization. They acted as wood-wards and the protectors of animals, and – like the Sumerian hero, Enkidu – they were untamed, speaking the instinctive language of nature with the ease of an animal. They were alternately perceived as admirable and threatening – admirable for their ability to sustain themselves outside the civilized world, and threatening because of the way they guarded their territory against the inroads of the town and city. The Green Man himself may still be seen in this way: he can be either friendly or aggressive according to how humanity behaves towards the environment.

In certain parts of Europe, especially Austria and Germany, the presence of the Wildman remains a part of the celebrations of the folk-year, and men clothed in costumes of leaves or mosses wander the streets of towns and villages and engage in mock combat with representatives of the summer.

GREEN DANCERS

When the rioting green of spring shouts in the woods and fields, no one can be still and silent, and in many parts of the world dances are performed in celebration of the new green. In Europe, and especially in Britain, teams of men dressed in white (or sometimes green) clothing, and carrying sticks and kerchiefs, gather to dance a variety of elaborate steps to the accompaniment of fiddle or accordion. This kind of folk-dance is known as Morris dancing, and though its origins are vague it almost certainly dates back to a time before the Middle Ages.

At one point in the display the Morris dancers perform a traditional sword dance, weaving long, flexible blades in and out in an

41

astonishing demonstration of skill. Finally, their weapons are woven into the shape of a six-pointed star called a 'knot'. With this they mime cutting off the head of one of their number, all the time crying 'A nut! A nut!'

This cry probably refers to the ancient symbol of the Knot of Wisdom, also known as the Pentangle or Solomon's Seal, a magical sign with origins of great antiquity. The fact that this same symbol was emblazoned on Sir Gawain's shield when

This Wildman leads a group of moss-clad dancers at the Austrian Perchtenlauf festival on Twelfth Night.

he encountered the Green Knight suggests a complex set of connections between the Green Knight's beheading game, the death of the Year King and the tests and trials of the Green Man.

But these spring dances also have the effect of reawakening the green life of the land: the striking of heel and sole upon the earth reminds the earth to be active; the striking of the Morris dancers' staves – reminiscent of fighting stags – reminds all living things that it is time to re-engage with life once more in an active way.

This, too, is the message of the Green Man, who invites and challenges us to rejoin him in the ongoing dance of the seasons, to acknowledge and celebrate the strength of greenness and its ability to transform us – and our lives – into something far richer and sweeter.

'celebrate the strength of greenness and its ability to transform us'

PART THREE

The Return of the Green Man

LEFT *The watchful head of the Green Man keeps an eye on visitors to the Gardens of Heligan, Cornwall, England.*

Leaves grow from mouth and eyes in this curious Green Man from the Church of St Michael, Spreyton, Devon, England.

In our own time, the Green Man has returned through a resurgence of interest in 'green' living, and increasing concerns for the survival of our natural habitat. Even the works of contemporary fantasists, such as the immensely popular *Mythago* novels of Robert Holdstock, or the urban fantasies of Charles de Lint, reflect a growing interest in the story of the Green Man. The character of Treebeard in J.R.R. Tolkien's phenomenally successful *Lord of the Rings* has brought his presence into the lives of countless readers, while comic-book heroes such as Green Lantern, Green Arrow and Slaine, and the popular TV series *Robin of Sherwood* – not to mention numerous Hollywood movies on the adventures of Robin Hood – have helped to keep us aware of the character and purpose of the Green Man in some of his many guises.

The challenges offered by the Green Man draw us back to a realization of our own perilously eroded relationship with the environment. A desire to conquer the natural world, to rob it of its resources, to decimate its productivity in the name of progress and financial gain, has caused us to come dangerously close to the destruction of the natural world. Today's return of the Green Man as an unacknowledged icon of the ecological movement can be seen as only the latest chapter in an age-old story which begins in the shadowy forest world of early man, and continues to this day in the ongoing struggle to save the green world from eventual extinction.

It is hardly suprising to come across him, emerging from the earth itself, amid the restored gardens at Heligan, Cornwall, or to find his spirit evoked close by in the dramatic Eden Project, where all the plant habitats of the world are represented in their own biospheres. As long as the spirit of restoration and rejuvenation of the earth goes on, the Green Man's presence will continue to be felt by all who love both the wilderness and the bright formal gardens of the world.

'the ancient respect for the green is being recovered'

REDISCOVERING THE GREEN

In a time when the world's tree cover is being steadily eroded, the ancient respect for the green is being recovered, not only as a spiritual, but also as a practical, necessity. Trees stabilize the atmosphere, exuding the oxygen that earth's living beings need to exist. Our symbiotic partnership with the green world is in the air we breathe, for the carbon dioxide which we exhale is processed by the trees. The Green Man's domain is also ours. Mythic and historic knowledge need the

47

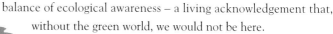

balance of ecological awareness – a living acknowledgement that, without the green world, we would not be here.

Nature's wisdom is an oral tradition which we can all experience. It is to the greenwood that we look to provide the paper on which to record our own store of wisdom in book form. We still need the nurture of the green, through the grains, nuts and fruits that it provides. We cover our bodies with clothes derived from the wood-pulp and fibres of the green world, coloured by vegetable dyes. The power of herbs, plants and trees restores us to health when we are sick. Truly, there is no end to our symbiotic connection with the green.

As once the Egyptians referred to good deeds as 'doing green things', so now we speak of 'being green' when we have the planet's well-being in mind. The message of the Green Man is not only a way of sharpening our awareness of the world around us, a heritage of myth and custom, but it can also touch the soul. As we travel further from daily contact with nature, there are practices that can help reconnect us, ways that bring a sense of proportion and belonging to lives that have become too ordered and civilized. As Shakespeare said, 'One touch of nature makes the whole world kin.' We are part of the family of life, perhaps not too proud to call the green our kindred.

'without the green world, we would not be here'

Celebrating the Green Man

The spirit of the Green Man can be invoked in a number of ways and he can easily become a focus for all kinds of activities in your life. You can use reproductions of foliate heads or other images of the Green Man (generally available in garden centres and gift shops) as the centre of a shrine which honours your relationship to the ancient Spirit of Nature and celebrates his dynamic presence in your life. Whether you choose to make a shrine for him in your garden or inside your home, his strong and earthy influence can add much to the daily rhythm of your life. What follows are a few suggestions of ways in which you may invite the Green Man to be a permanent presence in your life.

At Home

Unlike our ancestors, who spent much of their time outside, we live so much indoors that it helps to remember how much we depend on the green world for the air that we breathe, the materials and fibres that create implements, buildings, clothes, and give us the food that we eat. We are part of a delicate chain of life. Giving the Green Man a special place of honour in the home acknowledges our relationship to the green world. Nearly every home has a special place where plants flourish. The Green Man might want to live near this place, or be incorporated into a shrine made up of plants, flowers or dried grasses and leafy branches, depending upon the season. Seasonal shrines can be changed to keep the remembrance fresh: in spring, a bowl of hyacinths or spring flowers; in autumn, a vase full of corn stooks or grasses. And don't forget – the Green Man likes living, growing things rather than cut flowers!

Some people choose to set up the Green Man as a guardian of the home, his face becoming a welcoming and familiar friend when you come home – or a fierce deterrent for those who might be less welcome.

In the Office

The workplace doesn't have to be devoid of beauty or meaning. Whether you have an open-plan office or a private one, you can remember the green life of nature by placing an image of the Green Man in a space that you can call your own. If you have room, have an office plant as his special home, where he peers out between the leaves, perhaps standing on a stone. You are unlikely to be asked who he is and what he is doing there; if you are, then point out he is your mascot and has as much right to live on your desk as your boss's family photos or your colleagues' desk-toys! In the aridity of the urban workplace, everyone is able to share in the blessing of the green.

In the Garden

Those who enjoy gardening, and even those who only have a window-box or patio to be proud of, can set aside a place for the Green Man's Garden – an area in which special plants and stones can be positioned to create a green shrine. This is one of the Green Man's favourite places to be – out in the living world among the growing things!

In Groups and Communities

Wherever groups and communities come together in a shared environment or designated space, it is important that everyone respects the common areas, whether young or old. You can set an image of the Green Man in a place where he looks out over the communal areas in a protective way. If there are problems with tidiness or respect for the house, you could even draw attention to the situation without being too heavy-handed or officious by leaving a note as if from the Green Man. You may be surprised at the results it brings.

In the Sickroom or Hospital

One of the worst deprivations for those confined to bed for a long period is the disconnection with the world of nature. Though we long to rise and enjoy a walk, we may well be stuck indoors for interminable amounts of time that simply drag by.

The placement of a Green Man near the bed, or on a bedside shrine, reminds the patient that the green round of nature goes on, even though they may be far from its touch.

Ceremonies of Beginning

When you begin something – a new business enterprise or project, leaving home for the first time, passing an exam that qualifies you for a better position – the Green Man can be the focus of a simple ceremony of affirmation that dedicates your energies to the new idea moving through your life. If you are about to undertake some new and important task, make a dedication to the Green Man and ask for the energy to bring your desire to fruition.

Rededication Ceremonies

The Green Man is an especially important focus when fresh beginnings are made after difficult times. Whether it be a divorce or a period of recovery after a long illness, or the digging-over of a derelict garden or the clearance of a house after a death, use the Green Man to clear and bless whatever is passing, and to rededicate and bless whatever is coming into focus now. Just as the year turns, so, too, our lives can be brought to fresh life, and begin flowering again.

Harvest Ceremonies

The Green Man likes to be honoured by being given a central place at harvest ceremonies and blessings of the first fruits of the earth. If your garden has produced its first crop of runner beans or tomatoes, don't forget to offer a bean or tomato to him for his very own.

A Guardian of Animals

When our beloved pets die we often bury them in the garden. Whichever area you designate for this, you can set a Green Man head into a wall nearby or make a rockery or shrine over the place where your pet is buried. As the body passes back into the earth, so the plants that grow over them draw life and meaning from death. In this way you recall deities (such as Cernunnos, the Celtic 'lord of the animals') who have a deep and lasting connection as guardians of the animals.

Gift Giving

The Green Man makes a lovely gift between friends whose friendship is just beginning to grow, like the green leaves of the forest or the grain in the fields. To give an icon such as this emphasizes the harvest of friendship to come, as well as acknowledging the life-giving love that nourishes you both.

A Walking Meditation

Take yourself to a place in nature where you can walk. A park is fine, if you're in a big city; if you're in the country, the world is your oyster. When you are ready to begin your meditation, find a suitable place where you can start: a gateway, between a pair of trees, through a set of overarching branches – you decide. Let go of anxieties, and focus upon one pressing concern that you are going to take to the solution of nature for the duration of your walk. Your intention is to seek connection with the green life of nature and ask for help or guidance about your issue, so think about this before you step forward and ask for that help.

Begin your walk, noticing whatever comes to your attention as you go. Sometimes, a particular plant, the shape of a cloud, the song of a bird, the rustle of a bush, the apparition of a butterfly or the smell of a flower can be the messengers of nature. When something strikes you deeply, stop and consider it, relating it to the issue in your heart. Don't try to figure out what anything means – just accept it and hold it loosely in your heart and mind. The trick is to be receptive to your surroundings and to acknowledge them respectfully, just as you might greet a person you meet upon the road. Each element of the natural world can mirror – and help you reflect upon – what moves you.

Continue your walk until you feel that you've come to the end. You'll have a good sense of this. Before you go home, give thanks for the help you've received, even though your conscious mind may not have a clear or rational grasp on what has happened. You will notice that you have an altered perspective on your issue and that, in the next few days, you will feel differently, and perhaps begin to feel your way to solution.

Travels of the Green Man

A GAZETTEER

Representations of the Green Man can be seen and visited all over Europe, especially in France, Germany and Holland, where countless depictions of his leafy head peer down from the roofs of cathedrals and churches. Some of the finest examples are to be found in St Chapelle, Paris, the Church of St Bravo in Holland, the Kutná Hora Cathedral in the Czech Republic (there are also numerous Green Man faces on the houses in Prague) and at the Monastery Church of Altenburg in Germany. There are also a number of notable Green Men in Spain and Italy, where they can be found on the cathedral at Avila and the Doges Palace in Venice. Even in Russia, the cathedral of St Dimitri at Vladimir has a frieze of Green Men around one of its doors.

But the Green Man is by no means a purely European phenomenon. Since he represents the energy of the natural world, his image is to be found in many countries. Some of the earliest recorded images of his leafy face are found in modern-day Jordan, Lebanon and Tunisia, possibly deriving from the ancient Mesopotamian culture which once flourished there. Elsewhere, in

OPPOSITE *A colourful fourteenth-century foliate head frowns down from the rooftree of Exeter Cathedral, England.*

55

This scene from the Ball Court at Chichén Itzá, Mexico, shows a beheaded figure from whose neck sprout leaves.

Borneo, a consistent symbol of good luck and fertility is a face which sprouts roots and flowers. Known as Kirtimukha, this appearance of the Green Man is an ancient vegetation god who is also found carved into temples of the Jain religion throughout India. One of the finest Jain temples, at Ranakpur, is designed as a forest in stone, not unlike the cathedrals of Europe, and several Green Man-like faces can be seen amid the leaves.

Further afield still, on the American continent, some extraordinary images of the Green Man are to be found. In Mexico, where the ancient Mayan and Aztec cultures once flourished, there are some powerful representations of the Green Man. In the Ball Court at Chichén Itzá, for example, a decapitated body sprouts green leaves from its neck, while elsewhere at Uxmal, the Pyramid of the Magicians sports numerous foliate heads among a riot of carved foliage. The west front, north screen, reredos and sanctuary of the cathedral of San Francisco Javier at Tepoztlan, shows that the Green Man was adopted – here as elsewhere – by Christian architects.

This twelfth-century Green Man mask looks out from the North Chapel of Le Mans Cathedral, France.

For those who want to go in search of the Green Man for themselves, a list of some of the best examples throughout the world now follows (NOTE: for all entries where no specific site is listed, the building in question is simply the parish church). Only a fraction of the vast number of carvings and representations of the Green Man are listed here, and everyone has their favourites. I have tried to choose the most widely representative images from the many hundreds which exist. More are being discovered daily. I am greatly indebted to the work of Clive Hicks, Peter Hill and Ronald Millar, whose books offer more extensive listings than are possible here (see *Further Reading*, page 64, for details).

57

EUROPE

ENGLAND AND WALES

• **Buckinghamshire**
Langley Marsh, St Mary the
Virgin: *Corbels*
Leckhampstead, Church of the
Assumption: *Font panel*

• **Cambridgeshire**
Cambridge:
Pembroke College: *Corbel*
Queen College: *Wood carving*
St John's College: *Misericord*
Ely Cathedral Lady Chapel:
Roof bosses
Great Shelford, St Mary: *Porch boss*

• **Cheshire**
Astbury, St Mary: *Roof boss*
Chester Cathedral: *Misericord*
Nantwich, St Mary: *Stained glass*

• **Cornwall**
Bodmin, St Petroc: *Corbel*
Lostwithiel, St Bartholomew: *Font*
St Beryn, St Buriana: *Screen panels*

• **Devon**
Exeter Cathedral: *Numerous examples*
George Nympton, St Martin:
Roof bosses
King's Nympton, St Martin:
Roof bosses
Nymet Tracy, St Martin: *Roof bosses*
Sampford Courtenay, St Andrew:
Roof bosses
South Molton, St Mary Magdalene:
Corbel
Spreyton, St Michael: *Roof bosses*

• **Gloucestershire**
Elkstone, St John: *Tympanum*
Gloucester Cathedral: *Roof bosses*

• **Hampshire**
Winchester Cathedral:
Choir-stall spandrels

• **Herefordshire**
Bosbury, Holy Trinity: *Monument*
Hereford Cathedral: *Lintel carving*
Kilpeck, St Mary and St David:
Doorway
Much Marcle, St Bartholomew:
Capitals

• **Lancashire**
Cartmel Priory: *Choir stalls*
Whalley, St Mary and All Saints:
Misericord

• **Lincolnshire**
Cadney, All Saints: *Corbels*
Crowland Abbey: *Roof boss*
Grantham, St Wulfram: *Corbel*
Lincoln Cathedral: *Misericord*
Stamford, St John: *Roof boss*

• **Monmouthshire (Gwent)**
Llangwm, St Jerome: *Corbel*
Llantilio Crossenney, St Teilo: *Carving*

• **Norfolk**
King's Lynn, St Margaret: *Misericord*
Norwich Cathedral:
Roof bosses, misericord
Weston Longville, All Saints:
Sedilia arches

• **Northamptonshire**
Castor, St Kyneburga: *Capitals*
Wadenhoe, St Mary: *Corbel*

• **Nottinghamshire**
Newark, St Mary Magdalene:
Misericords, capitals
Southwell Minster:
Misericord, tympanum

• **Oxfordshire**
Abingdon, St Nicholas: *Corbel*

Dorchester Abbey: *Corbel*
Oxford:
    All Souls College: *Corbels*
    Exeter College: *Corbels*
    Magdalen College: *Corbels, capital*
    Merton College: *Corbels*
    New College: *Corbels, misericords*

- **Powys**
Machynlleth, Pennell Church:
    Stained glass

- **Shropshire**
Linley, St Leonard: *Tympanum*
Ludlow, St Laurence: *Misericord*

- **Somerset**
Bishops Lydeard, St Mary:
    Bench ends
Bristol, St Mary Redcliffe:
    Roof boss, corbel
Crowcombe, Holy Ghost: *Bench ends*
Queen Camel, St Barnabus: *Roof boss*

- **Staffordshire**
Lichfield Cathedral: *Capital*

- **Suffolk**
Mildenhall, St Mary: *Porch boss*

- **Warwickshire**
Coventry, Holy Trinity: *Misericord*

- **West Sussex**
Steyning Post Office: *Roof beam*

- **Wiltshire**
Sutton Benger, All Saints:
    Roof boss

- **Yorkshire**
Beverley Minster: *Capitals*
Fountains Abbey: *Window carvings*
Loversall, St Katherine: *Misericord*
Ripon Cathedral: *Corbels*

SCOTLAND

- **Lothian**
Aberlady Churchyard: *Gravestone*
Corstorphine Graveyard:
    Gravestone
Dalmany Church: *Capitals*

- **Roxborough**
Edinburgh, Roslin Chapel:
    Roof bosses, corbels
Melrose Abbey Museum:
    Rood-screen boss

IRELAND

- **Galway**
Clonfert Cathedral: *Fragments*
Galway, St Nicholas: *Window stop*

- **Kerry**
Aghadoe Church: *Carving*
Kilkenny Cathedral: *Corbels, panel*

- **Laois**
Killeshin, St Nicholas: *Window stop*

- **Offaly**
Clonmacnoise Cathedral: *Frieze*

- **Tipperary**
Cashel, Cormac's Chapel: *Capital*

AUSTRIA

Salzburg, Franciscan Church:
    Capital
Vienna, St Stephen: *Doorway*

BELGIUM

Antwerp Cathedral: *Corbel*
Bruges, Belfry: *Tower base*
Brussels Cathedral: *Vault boss*
Ghent Cathedral: *Roof bosses*
Liège Cathedral: *Misericords*
Tournai Cathedral: *Capitals*

BULGARIA

Melnik Rozhen Monastery:
    Green Man face

CYPRUS

Bellapaix Monastery: *Corbels*

CZECH REPUBLIC

Kladruby Monastery: *Entrance arch*
Kutná Hora Cathedral:
   Bench ends, bosses
Prague Cathedral: *Roof bosses*

FRANCE

Bordeaux Cathedral: *Capital*
Bourg-Lastic: *Capitals*
Brive-la-Gaillarde, St Martin: *Corbels*
Chanteuges: *Capitals*
Cherval: *Choir stalls, capital*
Cliltel-Montagne: *Capitals*
Issoire: *Capitals*
Le Mans Cathedral: *Capitals, bosses*
Le Puy Cathedral: *Capitals*
Marsat: *Corbel*
Mérignac: *Frieze*
Orcival: *Capitals*
Orl, St Aignan-sur-Cher:
   Capitals, porch, door
Paris:
   Louvre: *Roman sarcophagus*
   Musée Paris: *Capitals, stained glass*
   Notre Dame: *Capitals, stained glass*
   Place Vendome: *Keystones*

St Chapelle: *Capitals*
Poitiers Cathedral: *Capital*
Reims Cathedral: *West screen panels*
St Jean-de-Cole: *Apse, window capitals*
Thaims: *Capitals*
Thiers Abbey: *Capital*
Trizay: *Capitals*

Worms Cathedral, Germany

GERMANY

Altenburg: *Capitals*
Annaberg: *Bosses*
Bamberg Cathedral: *Corbel*
Brandenburg: *Vault paintings*
Braunschweig: *Bosses*
Cologne Cathedral: *Masks*
Hildesheim:
   St Gothard: *Capitals*
   St Michael: *Capital*
Königslutter am Elm: *Capitals*
Magdeburg Cathedral: *Bosses, capitals*
Munich, St Lukas: *Capitals*
Pfalzfeld: *Pillar of St Goar*
Regensburg Cathedral: *Bosses*
Schwäbisch Gmünd: *Horned faces*
Trier Cathedral: *Bosses*
Ulm Cathedral: *Corbels (Green Women)*
Wittenburg: *Capitals*
Worms Cathedral: *Corbels*

HOLLAND

Amsterdam, Rijksmuseum: *Carvings*
Den Haag, Royal Palace: *Keystones*
Haarlem, St Bavo: *Misericord, window*
Maastricht Basilica: *Wildmen carving*
St Hertogenbosch Cathedral:
   Bosses, capitals
Utrecht Cathedral:
   Capital, Wildman
Utrecht, St Peter: *Corbels*

HUNGARY

E. Budapest, Matthias Church:
   Capitals
Sopron Monastery: *Capital*

ITALY

Assisi Church: *Capital*

Florence:
    Medici Chapel:
        Frieze by Michelangelo
    Palazzo Vecchio:
        Courtyard, paintings
    Pitti Palace:
        Frieze, paintings, tapestry
    San Lorenzo: *Pulpit by Donatello*
Orta, S. Giulio: *Panel*
Pavia, San Michele: *Capital*
Rome:
    St Peter's Square:
        Fountain with leaf masks
    Via della Scipioni: *Capitals*
Venice, Doges Palace:
    Numerous capitals

MALTA

Mdina Museum: *Organ screen*
Valletta Cathedral: *Wall decorations*
Valletta, Palace Square: *Fountain*

NORWAY

Hurum, Valdres: *Wooden capital*
Rennebu, Sor-Trondelag:
    Portal, carved columns

RUSSIA

Vladimir, S. Dmitri: *Frieze around door*

Assisi Church, Italy

SPAIN

Avila Cathedral: *Wildmen, west front*
Barcelona, Santa Maria de Maria:
    Capitals, misericords
Córdoba Cathedral: *Choir woodwork*
León Cathedral: *Carvings, corbels*
Toledo Cathedral: *Outer decorations*

SWEDEN

Boge: *Capital*
Gothem: *Portal*
Gudheim Abbey: *Portal*
Linköping Cathedral: *Bosses, capitals*
Örebro, Nikolai Church: *Capitals*
Skara Cathedral: *Bosses*
Spoge: *Capitals*
Uppsala Cathedral: *Capitals*
Visby Cathedral: *Capitals*

SWITZERLAND

Payerne: *Bosses*
Sion Cathedral: *Bosses*

TURKEY

Ephesus, Temple of Hadrian:
    Roman capitals
Istanbul, Archaeological Museum:
    Roman capitals

61

The East

Near East/Africa

• **Jordan**
Khirbat-Al-Mafjir:
  Roman coffered ceiling

• **Lebanon**
Baalbek:
  Leafy Bacchus, temple frieze

• **Tunisia**
El Djem, Sousse Museum:
  Roman mosaic

Borneo

Apo Kayan Area:
  Numerous depictions of Kirtimukha

India

Dankhar Temple: *Wall paintings*
Delhi, Qutb Minar:
  Kirtimukhas on capitals
Delhi, National Museum: *Foliate heads*
Rajasthan Temple: *Foliate heads*

Rajasthan, Ranakpur (Jain Temple):
  Kirtimukhas

Indonesia

Borobudur Temple:
  Faces disgorging foliage

Nepal

Kathmandu, Swayambunath Temple:
  Numerous foliate heads

The Americas

Brazil

Sao Paulo, National Museum:
  Masks throughout gardens

Mexico

Chichén Itzá, Ball Court:
  Decapitated figure sprouting foliage
Mérida, Casa di Montilo:
  Green Men, Wildmen
Mérida Museum: *Carvings*
Mexico City: *Carvings on buildings*
Oaxaca Cathedral: *Panels*

Oaxaca, Santo Domingo:
  Pedestal beneath virgin
Tepoztlan, San Francisco Javier:
  Numerous carvings
Uxmal, Pyramid of the Magician:
  Heads entwined with foliage

USA and Canada

There are a surprising number of
Green Men depicted on some of the
older buildings (for New York reference,
see Stephen and Fitzgerald King's
book *Nightmares in the Sky* – details

in Further Reading, page 64). Here
are some examples:

West 75th St and Columbus: *Heads*
West 76th St and Columbus: *Heads*
West 80th St and Amsterdam: *Heads*
West 81st St and Columbus: *Heads*
West 84th St and Riverside: *Heads*
West 87th St and Columbus: *Heads*
West 88th St and Amsterdam: *Mask*
Toronto University: *Heads*

Sightings

Green Men are not hard to find, especially in Europe. The following table lists a number of events across England where you will certainly catch sight of masked and leaf-clad figures, with some notable events from other countries listed below.

Location	Event	Date
Cambridgeshire, Whittlesey	Straw Bear Festival	*Early January*
Cheshire, Knutsford	Royal Festival	*May Day*
Cornwall, Helston	Furry Dance	*8 May*
Cornwall, Padstow	Padstow Festival	*30 April*
Derbyshire, Castleton	Garland Day	*29 May*
Devon, Barnstaple	Green Man Procession	*New Year*
Devon, Pilton	Pilton Festival & Green Man Day	*Mid-July*
Essex, Thaxted	Thaxted Morris Ring	*Early Summer*
Kent, Rochester	Sweeps Festival	*May Day Holiday*
London, Deptford & City	Jack-in-the-Green Parade	*1 May*
London, Ealing, Brentham	May Day with Jack-in-the-Green	*2 or 3 May*
London, Walthamstow	Jack-in-the-Green.	*1 May*
Oxfordshire, Charlton-on-Otmoor	May Cross	*May Day*
Shropshire, Aston-on-Clun	Arbor Day	*29 May*
Shropshire, Clun	Green Man Day	*May Day Holiday*
Sussex, Hastings	Jack-in-the-Green Festival	*May Day Holiday*
Warwickshire, Aston Cantlow	Green Man's Midsummer Marriage	*Early June*
Warwickshire, Forest of Arden	Green Man Festival	*Mid June*

- **Austria:** *Grödig:* The Meeting of the Seasons, October / *Pongau district:* Perchtenlauf, Twelfth Night

- **Belgium:** *Rutten:* May Festivities, May

- **France:** *Auvergne, Chanteuges:* May Hunt, Whitsun

- **Germany:** Maypoles are to be seen everywhere throughout the summer

- **Mexico:** *San Pablito, Puebla:* Bark silhouettes of human foliage-figures are carried during crop fertility rituals

- **Scotland:** *Queensferry, Edinburgh:* Burryman Parade, Early August

- **Switzerland:** *Basle:* Wilde Mann, January / *Effingen:* Eirleiset, April / *Urnäsch:* Silvesterklause, New Year

Further Reading

Alexander, M. *British Folklore, Myths and Legends.* London: Weidenfeld & Nicholson, 1982

Anderson, W. *Green Man: The Archetype of our Oneness with the Earth.* London: Harper Collins, 1990

Basford, K. *The Green Man.* Cambridge: Boydell & Brewer, 1978

Cave, C.J.P. *Roof Bosses in Medieval Churches.* Cambridge University Press, 1948

Harding, Mike. *A Little Book of the Green Man.* London: Aurum Press, 1998

Harrison, Robert Pogue. Forests: *The Shadow of Civilization.* University of Chicago Press, 1992

Hicks, Clive. *The Green Man: A Field Guide.* Helhoughton, Fakenham: Compass Books, 2000

Hill, Peter. *In Search of the Green Man in Northamptonshire.* Orman, 1996

Husband, T. *The Wild Man: Medieval Myth & Symbolism.* Metropolitan Museum of New York

Hutton, Ronald. *The Stations of the Sun: A History of the Ritual Year in Britain.* Oxford University Press, 2001

James, E.O. *Seasonal Feasts & Festivals.* London: Thames & Hudson

Judge, R. *The Jack in the Green.* Boydell & Brewer/Roman & Littlefield, 1979

King, Stephen and Fitzgerald.

Nightmares in the Sky. New York & London: Viking Studio, 1988

Matthews, J. *Gawain, Knight of the Goddess.* London: Aquarian Press, 1990

Matthews, J. *Quest for the Green Man.* London/Wheaton, IL: Godsfield Press/Quest Books, 2001

Matthews, J. *Robin Hood: Green Lord of the Wildwood.* Glastonbury: Gothic Image Publications, 1996

Millar, Ronald. *The Green Man:*

Companion & Gazetteer. Seaford: SB Publications, 1997

Raglan, Lady J. *"The 'Green Man' in Church Architecture",* Folklore 50 (1939): 45–57

Sheridan, Ronald and Anne Ross. *Grotesques and Gargoyles: Paganism in the Medieval Church.* London: David and Charles, 1975

Wylie, Ruth. *"The Green Man/Foliate Head",* Folklore Society News, 24 (1999), pp11–12

Acknowledgements

The author wishes to acknowledge the work of that doyen of Green Man hunters, Clive Hicks.

Picture Credits

The AAA Collection: 41 / John Omerod 19 / Ronald Sheridan 7, 13 / Margaret Weller 56; The Art Archive: Marco Polo Gallery, Paris/Dagli Orti 16; BAL: Castle Museum & Art Gallery, Nottingham 28 / Louvre, Paris/Lauros-Giraudon 25; British Library: The Art Archive 22 / BAL 31; Britstock-IFA: Oliver Bolch/ HAGA 42; Fortean Picture Library: Janet & Colin Bord 21, 40; Collections: Mike Kipling 10 / Robert Pilgrim 32, 37; Liz Eddison: box spine & back cover inset, 49; Charles Francis: book cover, 44; Sonia Halliday Photographs: 46 / Sonia Halliday & Bryan Knox 35 / Bryan Knox 27; Clive Hicks 4, 36, 54, 57; Stephen Marwood: box back cover c; Photogenes: Diana Morris box front cover, 1, 52–3; Charles Walker Photographic: 14, 39, 60; Werner Forman Archive: 8.

Eddison • Sadd Editions

Editorial Director *Ian Jackson*
Senior Editor *Tessa Monina*
Proofreader *Nikky Twyman*
Creative Director *Nick Eddison*
Art Director *Elaine Partington*
Senior Art Editor *Hayley Cove*
Picture Researcher *Diana Morris*
Production *Karyn Claridge and Charles James*

Green Man plaque original designed by Fleur Robertson